# Why people are reading and sharing
## *Millionaire Women . . .*

"This is must reading for any woman wanting a career and simultaneously keeping her family intact. Jeanne Hauer proves that 'you can have it all, after all.'"

ROBERT L. SHOOK, *New York Times* Bestseller Author

"*Millionaire Women* illustrates how opportunities, challenges and the pursuit of one's passion can result in business accomplishment beyond imagination . . . with words of wisdom that apply to any gender desiring to start a business venture."

PROFESSOR SUSAN KUZNIK, Baldwin Wallace College

"A book that women and men will find entertaining, educational and inspirational for their own personal success."

HAL BECKER, Author/Motivational Speaker

"*Millionaire Women* is truly inspiring for every woman with a dream. Hauer captures both the drive and personality of the women she profiles."

JUDITH MANSOUR, Editor, *Northern Ohio Live*

"The underlying message of the book is that with creative thinking, bold action, resourcefulness, and a positive approach, other women . . . can achieve great financial and personal success."

PROFESSOR DIANA BILIMORIA, Case Western Reserve University

"This book is a must read for women of all ages. These 16 real life examples will provide hope and prove that nothing is impossible. I will make sure that my four daughters receive a copy of this book."

MARVIN MONTGOMERY, Author/Speaker/Trainer

D1302286

# Millionaire Women

## SUCCESS SECRETS of SIXTEEN WHO MADE IT from HOME

JEANNE TORRENCE HAUER

Barrington Publishing
Shaker Heights, Ohio

Copyright © 2003 Jeanne Hauer

All rights reserved. No part of this publication may be reproduced or transmitted in any form or by any means, electronic or mechanical, including photocopy, recording, or any information storage and retrieval system, without permission in writing from the publisher.

Publisher's Cataloging-in-Publication Data:

Hauer, Jeanne Torrence.
    Millionaire women : success secrets of sixteen who
made it from home / by Jeanne Torrence Hauer.—1st ed.
      p. cm.
    Includes bibliographical references.

    1. Businesswomen—Biography.  2. Women-owned business
enterprises.  3. Home-based businesses.  4. Success in
business.  5. Entrepreneurship—Case studies.
  I. Title

HD6072.5.H38 2002                         338'.04'0820922
                                             QBI02-200381

ISBN: 0-9721081-0-6

Cover and interior designed by Sans Serif, Inc., Saline, Michigan
Cover photograph by Janet Century.
Printed in the U.S.A.

*Whatever you would do or dream, begin it.*
*Boldness has genius, power, magic in it.*
—Goethe

*This book is dedicated to all the young women of the world
who are coming into their own in life, especially
my daughters, Megan and Katie.*

# Special Thanks

This book could not have become a reality without the support and encouragement of many people, too numerous to mention in total. Special thanks goes out first and foremost to the 16 women profiled here who shared their life stories openly and willingly as an inspiration to other women. Their achievement and generosity have touched my heart.

This book, however, would not have moved from its over10-year state as a great concept to an actual printed form if it were not for my mentors, who encouraged me to write down a plan, find the best information, chunk up the work and make it happen. Accomplished business executives and published authors were my guides along the way including Joe LaGuardia, Kathy King, Vivian Bradbury, A'Lelia Bundles, Bob Shook, Hal Becker, Marvin Montgomery, Carolyn Dickson, Mel Kaufmann and Ted Schwarz.

I am truly grateful to my husband, Rick, my daughters, family and friends who excused my many absences to write copy after my day job and cheered me on to the finish line with their ideas, insights and encouragement. Special thanks to my sisters . . . to Rosemary Torrence, who served as first editor and kept me in line after grammatical leaps of faith and to Mary Jane Dike for her finance and computer expertise. I am also grateful to Karen Eisenhauer of the *Wall Street Journal* staff in Cleveland who asked me where she could buy a copy of the book when I saw her many years after I had first discussed writing such a work

*— Special Thanks —*

but before I had put pen to paper. For my parents and their commitment to education, and for all the many people who con-
tributed their enthusiasm and their ideas, please accept my
sincere thanks.

# Contents

# — Contents —

# Introduction

The Chinese have an ancient curse; "May you live in interesting times." The first time I heard this, as a young woman, it puzzled me. I love interesting times. In fact, boredom is the one thing I loathe in life. My life choices reflect my need for growth, change and intellectual stimulation. What was the meaning of this curse?

As the years passed, and my life became more complex with marriage, children, and career in the mix of commitments, I gradually understood what the Chinese were trying to say. The straightforward life patterns that our parent's lives followed do not exist in the same world today. There are certainly traditional life choices to be made, but the options that surround us offer a kaleidoscope of life directions. The simplicity of life prior to the technology boom narrowed our choices and our awareness that there may even be life choices at all. Earlier generations followed a more predictable life path.

A woman who is coming of age into adulthood today is confronted with choices in every area of her life:

- *To attend college or find a job after high school*
- *Cultural and lifestyle choices*
- *To marry or remain single*
- *To marry young or wait until later*
- *To have children or not*
- *How many children to have*
- *To continue a career after children*
- *To stay at home in the child rearing years*

- *Day care or at-home childcare options*
- *To find a career or life work that is fulfilling.*

The list goes on. This is just a start. A woman's values, dreams, goals and abilities are the drivers that will lead her to her ultimate life choices. But the choices are not always easy. One path followed will often keep other opportunities from becoming possible.

In my mind, the Chinese were half-right to call these "interesting times" a curse. We are in the midst of change at lightning speed in every area of our lives. It is a lot to absorb. Yet, these interesting times create opportunities for women that did not exist even 20 years ago at the same level. Opportunities that empower women and encourage their growth are everywhere you look in the United States and in many other countries today.

Sadly, that is not true with all women in the world. Inequity and crimes against women are legal in many third world countries where women are oppressed, often harmed, and treated as the property of their husbands. These conditions need to be acknowledged. They are tragic circumstances that beg for positive resolution and world response.

However, the focus of this book will be directed to contemporary women's lives in developed countries, including case studies from the United States, where my experience was gained as a woman in business, as well as a "stay at home mom", along with profiles of women entrepreneurs from Canada, Australia, Holland and South Africa who shared their stories and advice enthusiastically to help women readers achieve their own success.

My life canvas included the color and dimension of a college education, a satisfying career, marriage, and the birth of two beautiful daughters. In all, the picture looks like a fairly easy landscape to paint. But there have been many intricacies of life choices that I have dealt with to keep a balance of my goals and the needs and interests and those of my family and friends. Just as I have filled in the detail, I have watched and listened to countless other women who have struggled to find their way in an "interesting" world full of choices that can make or break your career, your family, or your happiness.

The many women I have met along the way inspired me to write this book. Their conversations about how to live their lives and be the best that they can be in a world full of sometimes confusing choices are the catalyst for my writing. What are the best, the smartest life choices for contemporary women? The answers to that question are as varied as the people answering the question. This book will not attempt to be the sourcebook to answer the many burning questions of the day.

What *Millionaire Women* will do is offer up a dialogue about some of the issues women face in leading a fully productive life today. The profiles of sixteen women who found their own way and became highly successful in business are shared to inspire others who may want to start a business of their own. The home-based setting where these ventures began was selected as a criterion that would open the thinking of every woman, no matter what her economic restrictions or family commitments.

In the eighty plus years since women were granted the right to vote through the Nineteenth Amendment to the United States Constitution, which passed in 1920, conditions have improved but are not equal for women who choose a business profession. This book will attempt to offer up inspiration, words of encouragement, life balance strategies, success secrets and business tips to the readers who will enjoy the challenges, the choices, the ups and downs, and the humor that are part of the interesting lives of the women featured here.

If business is not in the big picture of choices for some women readers, so be it. The choice to not seek employment is a viable one for many. Other professions and work as a stay at home mom may be the fully productive life a woman has chosen. In fact, I found my seven years as a "stay at home mom" to be some of the hardest, fully productive work I have ever done, and certainly the most important. The more traditional women career choices may not create the same need for new approaches as women in business may experience. But the women profiled here can be an inspiration to anyone. Their life canvasses may hang in the futuristic section of the world museum, as they have lead women into new areas, new horizons of opportunity that continue to present women with life choices for "interesting times."

Through the years, I have spoken with many women who have confided that they did not want to go back to the traditional career they were trained in, be it teaching, nursing or social work. They would love to find a small business interest or a new career. Often, they shared that they would like to do "something" where they could earn extra money from home. Some asked me for my advice.

I never had a great answer for these friends. Perhaps their other friends or their husbands and families have given them support or information that could help to identify a new path. The dialogue this book inspires will offer a message to those seekers who continue to search for a satisfying alternative. For other women who have a great idea and little encouragement, this book can be subtitled, "Don't Let Your Dreams Die at Home." But for all, it will be a message of courage, hope and encouragement for women as they find their own way.

Special recognition and my deepest gratitude goes out to the 16 women profiled in this book who shared their life stories willingly and with great generosity as a means to inspire other women to pursue their life goals. These pages will capture their stories as shared with me without attempt to verify their experience in specific detail.

A final note: a number of the Millionaire Women have asked me to clarify that their business was chosen because it hit one million dollars in annual sales, not because of any recorded net worth of the individuals. While I mention this in Chapter Three it bears mentioning here. These are stories of women who have reached for their full potential. The best of their stories are their measures of personal growth, above and beyond their financial growth or net worth, which were not criteria for inclusion or even known by this author. Please read this collection of life stories with that recognition in mind.

It has been my great privilege to get to know these high-achieving women over the course of writing this book. I hope you enjoy reading their stories as much as I have writing them.

# 1

# The Millionaire Fascination

*A* million bucks. A million smackers. A million dollars. No matter what you call it, one million dollars holds a special allure to almost everyone it seems. Even those who have many millions of dollars still hold that sum to be a precious commodity.

*The Millionaire* television program in the 1960's gave viewers a good look at the power of this amount of money as it was bestowed on a new recipient each week. A mysterious benefactor was behind the amazing, no-strings-attached gift.

The expression, "you look like a million bucks" has for many years been a compliment that was indeed high praise. What is the mystery or the impact of this number that keeps it in focus for all of us as a measure of someone who has made it big?

The term, *millionaire,* was reportedly coined in 1740, shortly before the formation of the United States. At the time of the European expansion on the new continent, fortunes of $1million were almost unheard of.

Over the years, the idea of becoming a millionaire had its own special glamour because it was almost impossible to achieve. The allure was woven into its elite exclusivity while it was associated with such names as Carnegie, Ford, and Vanderbilt. According to a May, 2000 report by Lincoln Financial Group, Mendelsohn Media Research Inc., Yankelovich Partners and Wirthlin Worldwide Inc., in 1948 one in 11,287 U.S. citizens was a millionaire, in contrast to one of every 359 Americans in 1983. Further, in 1974, there were 90,000 individual millionaires and about 350,000 millionaire households calculated by combined incomes in the United States. That was 0.5 percent of the population.

Today, a million dollars is a phenomenon within the realm of possibility for almost anyone with a bit of luck or good business skills. There are more United States millionaires than ever before.

Entertainers' and sports celebrities' millionaire status has become commonplace. Now, however, state lottery winners and Publisher's Clearing House Sweepstakes winning millionaires are being joined by game show winners from such hit quiz shows as *Who Wants To Be A Millionaire?* and *Greed,* along with, the *Survivor* series, where individuals pit themselves against nature and one another to win a million dollar cash prize. Survival of the fittest or the luckiest has created a special class of "the new rich".

The bizarre *Who Wants To Marry A Millionaire?* television special took this entertainment concept to a new low as producers attempted to create a wealthy "match made in heaven" for public consumption. Ratings aside, the union did not bind. Marrying for money, in this case, was a complete relationship disaster.

Savvy investors, who rode on the U.S. stock market's long bull run, have added their names to the millionaire list. In spite of economic changes, many remain in that category. There were five million millionaire individuals in the United States as of the year 2000, according to the recent research. This number is up from 3.5 million in 1996. Now, about one in 50 U.S. individuals has a net worth of one million dollars. Interesting to note is that people in every part of the country have achieved millionaire status, unlike a previous era when high net worth individuals were concentrated in New York, Boston, Chicago and other financial centers. Additional research by Merrill Lynch and Gemini Consulting reports that globally the wealth of millionaires worldwide is expected to leap by an annual 12 percent to $44.9 trillion by 2004.

Now that a million dollars in net worth is more achievable, we are bombarded with messages on the subject. Thomas J. Stanley's best sellers, *The Millionaire Next Door* and later, *The Millionaire Mind*, have peaked public interest in the subject and offered strategies to join the club of "prodigious accumulators of wealth." Mr. Stanley, in his first book on the subject, offers in-depth analysis of high net worth individuals. Intelligence, personality, career characteristics, consumption and investment patterns combine to paint a picture of America's self-made wealthy. *The Millionaire Mind* sequel zeroes in on America's wealthiest financial elite and draws the mental profile of this top tier. Social skills, courage, discipline, integrity, physical fitness, choice of spouse and investment strategies are among the factors he examines, that have an impact on high net worth individuals.

New books on millionaire topics are joined by the new dot com information explosion. *Millionaire Magazine* and its *millionaire.com* web site offer information, news, products, services, trips and reserved auction seating for upscale audiences who "want the very best the world has to offer." In fact, there are currently 1349 web sites on the Yahoo.com search engine with news about millionaires or information on how to make a million ourselves. *Millionaire Island, The Millionaire Kit, Millionaire Village, Millionaire Maker, Millionaire Madness, How to be a Millionaire, E Millionaires Club, Five Days to a Million, Armchair Millionaire,* and *Six-Figure Income* are among the sites that hold the most sizzle in the "how-to" category. One would think with this abundance of advice that great wealth can be achieved if we just sign up for a survey course or a lifetime subscription to the best on-line advisor's publication.

Just how much will a million buy in the second millennium? The consumer price index, which measures inflation and the cost of living, has risen 479 percent over the past 40 years. Today's one million dollars is equivalent to $173,000 in 1960 purchasing power. In other words, what you could buy for one million dollars forty years ago would cost you $5.8 million today.

In light of this, what do we know about one billion dollars? According to *Forbes* magazine, in 1982 there were thirteen billionaires in the United States. By 1995, *Forbes* listed 100 individuals with fortunes of more than a billion dollars. In 1999, there were 267 U.S. billionaires on record.

Regardless of the small increases in the billionaire ranks, the vast expanse between reaching for one billion or for one million dollars will likely keep us focused and fascinated with the first rung of the high net worth ladder, one million dollars.

# 2

# The First
# Woman Millionaire

*T*he first woman self-made millionaire in the United States was a black hair care entrepreneur who founded the Madam C. J. Walker Manufacturing Company in 1905. There has been much written of late about this unusual individual, although original historic accounts are limited. The most comprehensive and reliable account of her life has been recently released by A'Lelia Bundles, her great-great granddaughter who has compiled twenty years of research in the book, *On Her Own Ground: The Life and Times of Madam C.J. Walker (2001).*

Born in 1867 to parents Owen and Minerva, two years after the end of the Civil War, Sarah Breedlove started out her life with nothing. She was the fifth child born into the family and the first one born into freedom, just five years after the signing of the Emancipation Proclamation. Her parents were former slaves turned sharecroppers living on a Delta, Louisiana cotton plantation. Sarah was orphaned at age seven and completed very little traditional schooling. Poor cotton crops forced Sarah and her older sister, Louvenia, to move to Vicksburg, Mississippi and earn a living by washing clothes.

At age fourteen, Sarah married Moses McWilliams. Three years later, in 1885, she gave birth to a baby girl, Lelia. According to all reports, the birth of her daughter gave new spirit and resolve to Sarah in spite of the continued difficult circumstances of her life. Although specific historic detail is limited, in 1888, when Sarah was 20 years old she was widowed. Exact details of Moses' death are unknown.

Determined to survive her difficult life circumstances, Sarah moved to St. Louis, Missouri to start a new life with her daughter. There she enjoyed the closeness of her brothers, Alexander and James, who had moved to that city previously and worked as self-employed barbers.

Sarah continued to work as a laundress for nearly 20 more years. During her years in St. Louis, she learned much about life in a big city and the inner workings of society and power. Her involvement at the St. Paul African Methodist Episcopal Church would become the hub of her social life and a strong support system for a single woman raising a child alone. Her exposure at church and at work to the comfort of the middle and upper class in St. Louis left Sarah longing to escape the drudgery of her current life as a laundress. She prayed for strength to find a means to realize her dreams and free Lelia from a similar grim fate. Living on scanty means, Sarah moved often. For months at a time, she lived with one of her brothers, just steps away from facing homelessness depending upon her current employment situation.

In August of 1894, Sarah married John Davis, hoping that this union would bring to her and Lelia a measure of stability, comfort and respectability. Unfortunately, the union was a poor choice and Sarah's hopes were met with frustration, arguments and disappointment, as John did not provide for his new wife and child. In 1902, Lelia was enrolled in Knoxville College. Sarah willingly sent all the resources she could pull together to pay the $7.85 for her daughter's monthly room and board at school. With her daughter safely settled, Sarah was free to take control of her life. In 1903, the couple dissolved the union weeks just weeks before Sarah's thirty-sixth birthday.

At the conclusion of the tumultuous relationship with Davis, Sarah began seeing a man named Charles Joseph (C.J.) Walker, a newsman and advertising salesman for one of St. Louis three black newspapers. C.J. Walker was a man with whom she believed she could build a life. At that time, Sarah began several years of work on her own education and grooming, still seeking a path into a better life. She became more active in her church community.

By then, she was in her late 30's, and was having serious problems with her hair. Her scalp itched and her hair was breaking and falling out in patches, likely made worse by the stress of her life and the limited hygiene for hair that was common in that era.

Sarah sought relief in a number of available remedies, many of which were costly and fraudulent in their promises. During this time, she had occasion to meet Annie Minerva Pope-Turnbo, who was a purported hair expert. Pope-Turnbo taught Sarah and others the importance of cleanliness and hygiene. At the same time, she purchased and successfully used Pope-Turnbo's Wonderful Hair Grower remedy, which started to improve the health of Sarah's hair. Soon, she became an agent for the hair product and began to work as a hairdresser, an opportunity that doubled her weekly income. Still plagued with the quality of her own hair, Sarah experimented with various home remedies over the years.

In 1905, Sarah moved to Denver, Colorado, seeking a new start for her life and her aspirations. Shortly after, C.J. Walker joined her there and they were married. Sarah continued to sell the Wonderful Hair Grower in her Colorado life, and at the same time took a renewed interest in creating the perfect mixture to bring health, growth and texture to black women's hair. As legend goes, inspiration came to Sarah in a dream, along with the perfect formula for a hair product to cure her ailment. By her account a big black man appeared to her in a dream and told her what to mix, including a remedy from Africa. Sarah called her special concoction which contained sulfur, a centuries-old remedy for healing skin and scalp disease, Madam Walker's Wonderful Hair Grower.

Sarah had a hunch that she had a great product that would be in demand, much like Pope-Turnbo's had been. She mixed her first products in a washtub and sold her Wonderful Hair Grower from door to door. Soon after, her daughter, Lelia, would join her in Denver and in running the business.

Sarah's marriage to C. J. Walker gave new momentum to her sales efforts with his knack for promotion and sales. Community events were fertile ground for promotional events to illustrate Sarah Walker's then spectacular shoulder length hair growth. Major advertising campaigns in black newspapers built demand for the product. Sales agents were eventually trained to increase distribution. A mail order business was set up to meet demand.

In 1907, the Walker's left Denver and began an 18-month road trip to sell their product throughout the southern United States, spurred on to find new markets with larger market demand. That year, the business took in $3,652, nearly triple its previous year's earnings. At a time when most working black women made only $8 to $20 per month as domestic workers and white male factory workers made monthly incomes of $40 to $60 per month, Madam Walker's business was earning about $300 monthly, truly an impressive achievement.

In 1908, the couple decided to end their travels and attend to the mail order business that had expanded too quickly for long-distance management of the owners. They settled in Pittsburgh, Pennsylvania because of its easy access to shipping through rail service. Here the Walkers set up their business headquarters and Sarah opened the Walker Hair Parlor in the fashionable Hill District. In 1910, following a visit there, Sarah and C.J. moved their company headquarters again, this time to Indianapolis, Indiana. Five years later, she would move the business once again, this time to New York City, a move completed after her divorce from C.J. Walker.

Long hours, persistence, determination, a rigorous travel schedule and charitable work were the building blocks to her eventual great success. Over time, her company grew to include a factory employing 50 workers and more than 20,000 independent sales agents in the United States, Central America and the Caribbean. Most of these agents were women who sold her products and taught the Walker Hair Care Method.

Upon her death from kidney disease at age 51 in 1919,

Madam had built a fortune estimated at $600,000 to $1 million, which is equivalent to approximately $6 million today. Throughout her success, Madam was a generous philanthropist, contributing to organizations and causes she believed in including the YMCA, the NAACP's anti-lynching fund and black colleges and organizations. At this time, she is the only African-American woman in the United States National Business Hall of Fame.

Pioneering black educator, Mary McLeod Bethune wrote these words of comfort to Madam's daughter in memoriam: "Madam C. J. Walker's life was the clearest demonstration I know of a Negro woman's ability recorded in history. She has gone, but her work still lives and shall live as an inspiration to not only her race, but to the world." Looking back at the tremendous adversity faced by Madam C.J. Walker throughout her life, she is an incredible testimony to the power of persistence, vision and hard work in spite of seemingly insurmountable obstacles.

# 3

# *Women in Today's Land of Plenty*

**M**adam C. J. Walker, the first self-made woman millionaire, is an inspiration to every woman who has an interest in business. Her work in the early 1900s, despite great odds, and her eventual millionaire achievement are remarkable and truly unique.

The question arises, how are most women today doing in the land of plenty? As economists point to the great opportunity currently to earn millionaire status, how are women stacking up in the achievement of great wealth? According to Tom Stanley's research as reported in *The Millionaire Mind,* more than 90% of million-dollar net worth households are comprised of married couples where the main breadwinner is the husband. About half of the other 10% is made up of widows and widowers. While many women may be enjoying the wealth generated by a high earning husband, parity is not to be found at the highest levels in women's compensation.

The U.S. Department of Labor's March, 2000 report on "Trends for Women in the Workplace" notes that we have seen a steady increase of the number of women in the work force. There were 62 million workingwomen in 1999 with 75% employed full-time and 25% working half time. Women made up nearly half of the labor force and 53.5% of the professional ranks in 1999.

However, the report states that women overall earn about 76% of what men make annually. Further research points out that in top-paying professions, women earn only about 55% of what their male counterparts do. Occupations with the highest median weekly earnings for women in 1999 included (in descending income rank) pharmacists, lawyers, electrical and electronic engineers, computer system analysts, scientists, college/university teachers and physical therapists.

There is currently one woman for every five men who achieve a six-figure income. According to the U.S. Small Business Administration report, *Women in Business 2001,* only 5% of U.S. women executives earned more than $80,000 compared with 23% of male executives. Women make up less than 3% of senior managers in the nation's largest companies. Further findings from the *Women in Business 2001* report include:

- *Households headed by women tend to be poorer than those headed by men.*
- *The level of women's involvement in business management is*

*approaching that of men's, yet their personal earnings remain far below men's.*

- *Women-owned businesses as compared to those owned by men are more likely to be small and under five years old.*
- *Women received only 2.3 percent of total federal prime contracts in fiscal 2000.*
- *Women-owned businesses were more likely than their male counterparts to use personal credit cards to finance their business.*

Perhaps it is the lack of parity in the workplace that is driving the trend toward women starting their own businesses. Much has been written about "the glass ceiling" as a barrier holding down compensation and promotion for women in management. The growth of female-owned business startups seems to indicate that women are finding new doorways into the marketplace. The entrepreneurial approach of women, in response to limitations of traditional workplace opportunity, is evidenced in the rapid rate of growth of women-owned businesses.

According to the most recent U.S. Bureau of Labor Statistics figures, 3.8 million women list self-employment as their primary occupation. The Center for Women's Business, formerly the National Foundation for Women Business Owners, reports in their *Women Owned Business in 2002:*

- *Women-owned firms in the top 50 U.S. metropolitan areas number nearly 3.2 million.*
- *These same businesses employ more than 4.9 million people to generate more than $661 billion in total sales.*
- *Expansion of women-owned businesses with 100 or more employees and those with $1 million or more in revenues is outpacing the growth rate of all businesses of the same size.*

Between 1987 and 1996, the number of women-owned companies has grown 78 percent. Between 1997 and 2002, the Center estimates that the number of women-owned firms will have grown by another 14% and will stand at 6.2 million by the end of 2002.

While there has been some disparity among reporting agencies and research organizations, based on fundamental accounting parameters used to evaluate the exact total of women entrepreneurs, all research entities are recording extraordinary rates of growth. Economic forecasters predict that this momentum will continue as women are starting businesses now at twice the rate of their male counterparts.

Against the backdrop of the sobering statistics for women's accumulation of wealth in the traditional workplace, it is cause for great celebration when a woman-owned business achieves great success. This book, *Millionaire Women: Success Secrets of Sixteen Who Made It From Home,* will share the stories and success secrets of sixteen women entrepreneurs who started a home-based business that eventually hit one million dollars in annual sales.

Many of these were trailblazers, women entrepreneurs before there were role models for such life choices. All of them have hit the million-dollar sales mark in their business endeavors, an achievement that earned them a place in this book of inspirational stories. The personal net worth of these women was never researched and will remain confidential here, to be categorized only as high achieving and likely high net worth individuals.

Life stories of home-based business origin have been chosen to point out that great ideas can be spun into a new venture no matter where that business actually takes place. According to data from the U.S. Bureau of Census, more than 60% of women-owned businesses were operated in the home when they were first established.

Financial and/or family considerations may make home-based opportunities most attractive to many women. The sixteen Millionaire Women profiled here epitomize that creativity, drive, well-defined goals and a passion for your work can fuel a successful business venture, wherever it originates. A summary of their Success Secrets will offer their combined wisdom and common approaches to high achievement.

# 4

# The Pull to the Home

A discussion of the success stories and secrets of this group of Millionaire Women would not be complete without probing into why they began their businesses at home. In fact, why does any woman start a business from her home? The fact that more than 60% of women-owned businesses were launched from home makes one wonder, why?

The three main motivations for deciding upon a home base for a business appear to be cost, comfort and children.

## ▶ THE COST FACTOR

When a new product or service is moving from the idea stage into production, market planning and sales, it is often anyone's guess as to whether or not someone wants or needs it enough to pay for it. It might be an attractive item, but the market for it may be too small or production too costly to be priced for mass appeal.

A hypothetical example would be a case of a new battery-powered wagon. Such a wagon might be handy to own, but actual demand for an item like this could be limited. Cost to produce one unit could also make it comparatively expensive, which would tend to reduce the numbers of buyers as well. Until the "battery-wagon" is launched, an entrepreneur cannot know what the actual profit or available cash will be to sustain such a business. This case illustrates that when testing any new product, it is important to keep overhead and manufacturing expenses low to minimize the risk of losing money and maximize the financial resources for an effective product introduction.

A home-based venture uses a location of personal residence, which is available at no added cost, to serve double duty for a home and for a business. (There may be tax advantages gained in this scenario as well.) If a new product or service does not sell well, the business owner has avoided additional rent costs incurred by separate office or manufacturing space.

Lillian Vernon is a prime example of minimizing such financial risk. The multimillion-dollar Lillian Vernon Corporation grew from Lillian's early advertising and sales of monogrammed belts and handbags, work she cautiously strategized and distributed early on from the kitchen table in her home.

New business ventures often find it difficult to secure conventional bank financing. Financial institutions can be wary of new ideas, depending upon the concept and the availability of funding in a given economy. Nearly three-quarters of all women-owned firms accessed some type of credit in 1993. The U.S.

Small Business Administration reports that key issues for women-owned business, regardless of location, include maintaining business profitability, managing and maintaining business growth, managing cash flow, and keeping up with technology. All of these variables are cost-sensitive. A home-based business can at least curb extra cost in the facility area, leaving whatever financial resources are available for other critical needs.

## ▶ THE COMFORT ZONE

Many new companies begin as second income projects. Over time, the "little business on the side" can become so compelling or profitable that its owner decides to quit his or her day job and run the new entity full-time. A home base is the perfect location for a second business since much of the work is often completed after hours.

Two Men and A Truck was a little side business when it began. Founder, Mary Ellen Sheets, decided to quit her day job with the state of Michigan after several years of running the moving company with her evening and weekend personal time. Cost and comfort factors were reasons this business was well suited for its origins at home.

In the early years of any new venture, it is common for the founder to put in long hours, sometimes working well into the evenings to complete needed tasks. A home-based business enjoys the comforts of home in the midst of this demanding schedule. "Multi-tasking" is often the order of the day as women entrepreneurs handle household responsibilities on short breaks throughout their career workday. Flexibility and accessibility are benefits home workers enjoy whether business founders or employees.

Trend analysts at The Herman Group report that "earning a living at home has never been easier. Telecommuting has increased dramatically by corporations and in popularity with workers. More and more people will work from home, on flexible schedules, to respond to the expectations of employers, coworkers and customers around the globe. Home-based business is increasing, as people seek independence and influence over their success."

Telephone, fax, copiers, personal computers, video conferencing and the Internet have created a perfect environment for the "virtual office". Major corporations like Pfizer, Bell & Howell and Oracle are in line with many small home businesses, acknowledging that the home office can be the best location for a particular type of work in some situations. It is widely recognized today that with technological advances, the home office can offer convenience, comfort and economy without sacrificing efficiency for many companies or their field representatives.

▶ *WHO'S WATCHING THE KIDS?*

According to a 1997 study conducted by the Center for Women's Business Research, formerly the National Foundation of Women Business Owners (NFWBO), home-based women business owners in the United States are very similar to non home-based women business owners. They are not more likely to have children at home in contradiction to the theory that women base careers from home to balance the needs of work and a young family.

Statistics aside, women today are still generally considered the primary caregiver for children in a family setting. There are, of course, many more creative and nontraditional arrangements for child rearing than ever existed for previous generations. But, the work involved with having babies and raising children needs to be done by someone. More often than not, primary childcare responsibilities are a mother's work to handle personally or find a suitable substitute.

For years now, the debate has raged between "stay at home moms" and "working moms" over the relative advantages and pitfalls of either life choice. Quality childcare, early and later childhood development issues, economic factors, personal satisfaction and career commitments are among many variables that continue to surface in discussion of choices.

Support for the working choice may take the shape of flexible hours or on-site day care in the work place. Reinforcement for the stay-at-home option may present itself in neighborhood, church or on-line support groups. Mothers At Home (MAH), also known as the Family and Home Network, (www.mah.org) in Vienna, VA is the nation's largest and oldest national nonprofit organization supporting mothers who have chosen, or would like to choose, to be at home to nurture their families.

Former First Lady, Hilary Clinton, explores this state of affairs and the needs of children in her recently published book, *It Takes A Village*. She contends that we cannot return to the old world settings and need to find new creative solutions to allow for quality childrearing and meaningful work for women.

There are liberal voices from the left that hold that women have an equal right to work regardless of considerations of children. Family responsibilities are gender neutral in this scenario. From the extreme right, traditional conservative rhetoric pleads with women to stay at home, care for the children and reinforce traditional family values on a day-to-day basis.

In my experience, most women today operate somewhere in the middle of the debate, looking for the best solutions for their specific family circumstances. There are not black and white best answers. The baby years, preschool, elementary and high school years may require different approaches and choices over time.

This book is not a treatise on the debate that mothers must evaluate for themselves. These remarks are certainly not comprehensive or conclusive. What is key however, is the acknowledgment that raising children can be a factor in a decision to start a business from home. The potential to have greater interaction with children, to minimize added childcare costs, and to participate in meaningful employment from home may be the answer some women are seeking. The recently released book, *Mompreneurs*, by Ellen Parlapiano and Patricia Cobe offers ideas and strategies to start such a home-based business.

A version of the "stay-at-home" choice was the motivation for Lane Nemeth who founded Discovery Toys to afford herself flexible work hours and more time with her two-year old daughter, Tara. Lane's decision was in sync with her career work that was ultimately, helping parents raise brighter children through use of educational toys and products, such as those created and distributed by Discovery Toys.

In any case, for many women there is a pull to stay at home whether for cost, comfort or childcare considerations. In the following chapters, you will find stories of 16 women who used their homes as a base to begin a highly successful business. Their growth into Millionaire Women is an interesting evolution from any perspective.

> *"Family mealtime matters."*
>
> **Doris Christopher**

# The Pampered Chef

I have met Doris Christopher before. You may have also. She is the embodiment of the classic mom who worked as a teacher prior to raising children, stayed home once the kids were born, and later, wanted to do something in business after the youngest child went off to school. Women who have lived a life similar to Doris are a major inspiration for this book.

Her decision to stay home for eight years and then return to a business enterprise parallels the life choices of this book's author in many ways. What really sets Doris apart from the majority of former teachers, restless stay-at-home moms and others, is that she had a great idea that was in line with her personal and professional goals and she took the leap to start a home-based business on her own.

When Doris Christopher's youngest child reached kindergarten age, it appeared that there was now time in Doris' life to go back to work, perhaps part-time. There would still be plenty of family needs to be met, but the daily schedule afforded extra time that could be used to start saving for college and future family needs through Doris' work. She was fortunate that her husband had a respectable position in management with a Chicago company. But Doris wanted to contribute to the family income for her own growth and to make a difference in the their lifestyle.

Taking care of the family was still a definite priority. Part-time work would be ideal, but she knew it would be difficult if not impossible to find a relatively high level part-time position in the traditional workplace. She thought long and hard about what type of business would be possible to run from her home. A cooking school was considered, as Doris had been a home economics teacher in a secondary school. Catering was a possibility as she was an excellent cook. Caterers worked every holiday and weekend however, which was time that would be taken away from family needs. Other ideas were explored but none seemed to fit until Doris came upon the idea of starting a business selling high quality cooking tools.

In 1980, The Pampered Chef was born. It was the perfect

combination of business opportunity and personal scheduling to allow Doris to succeed in the new venture. Her background as a home economics teacher and later as a resource person for the University of Illinois, gave her the knowledge and skills as an expert in the cooking arena. A passion for cooking and culinary flair made this the perfect choice for enjoyable and meaningful work. Most important of all to Doris, this new enterprise would allow her to participate in the business arena while balancing the needs of her family.

## ▶ *"FAMILY MEALTIME MATTERS"*

"Family mealtime matters," is the underlying philosophy of the company's founder, its products and its sales staff. The kitchen tools that Doris selected for her collection would make work in the kitchen faster, easier and more fun and allow for a higher quality of cooking and at-home dining experience. Doris was committed to making family meals a focal point in her own family as a means to stay connected with one another and celebrate the victories of the day. Less time preparing meals would also leave families with more time to enjoy one another. The Pampered Chef products and recipes supported this basic philosophy of life.

In perfect alignment with her family values and product line is the choice of distribution that she selected for the kitchen collection. Doris decided to use home sales as the means of selling The Pampered Chef wares. By using this approach, she was able to offer an alternative to others who wanted to stay home with children and work a flexible schedule. A Pampered Chef career can easily be accomplished in this setting without putting family time or shared mealtimes at risk. By the same token, people who want to work full-time also have a great opportunity for career accomplishment.

### ▶ GRADUAL GROWTH

The Pampered Chef did not become a major company overnight, although the new products were quickly in great demand. The company started out with Doris running the business from a 400 square-foot area in the basement of her home. She found a number of kitchen tools that she thought appropriate for her line and began to host Kitchen Shows to present the products to new customers.

The early years were very much a family affair. Doris bought, tested and sold the products. She also created feature recipes and presented Kitchen Shows. Her husband, Jay, was responsible for the finances, packing, and shipping. Their two daughters, Julie and Kelley, helped by hand-stamping The Pampered Chef logo on paper bags for customer orders. Eventually, high school students were hired to help pack orders and inventory product after school. In the first two months of business, the new company saw $10,000 in sales.

In spring of 1981, one of Doris' friends asked if she could become a Kitchen Consultant and begin to host Kitchen Shows herself. After much consideration, Doris realized she could use the help and that the concept of an independent sales force would help the business grow more quickly. By the end of that year the company had 12 Kitchen Consultants along with temporary help for packing and shipping. In their first full year of operation they reached $100,000 in annual sales.

In the early years, Doris recalls that the company grew incrementally. It continued to operate in her home until 1985 when the business finally outgrew the basement space. That year, Doris and Jay were able to purchase a small suburban commercial building that was located not far from their home. The Pampered Chef used one of the 1,200 square-foot floors. A tenant rented the other floor from them. Four years later, the company relocated to larger quarters to accommodate its growth.

A series of moves to larger facilities would follow over the years. Today, the company operates from several locations with a total of 900,000 square feet for its operation. Soon, it will be moving to a new headquarters facility with over one million square feet of space and most operations functioning under one roof.

Word of mouth was the most powerful marketing tool that drove the business development early on. Doris grew the business gradually, moving from her local market to surrounding cities and states. Once the Chicago and surrounding Illinois markets were established, she spent time in Indianapolis, IN, St. Louis, MO, and Milwaukee, WI placing advertisements and recruiting Kitchen Consultants to represent her company throughout the Midwest. A major breakthrough came about in 1987 when *Family Circle* magazine featured The Pampered Chef in an article for its national readership. That publicity catapulted the company's growth throughout the United States.

Once the U.S. distribution network was established, the company expanded into Canada (1996), the United Kingdom (1999), and Germany (2000). Continued international growth is anticipated in the years ahead.

The net result of this continued growth over the past 21

years is an established company with a headquarters staff of 1,100 and more than 66,000 independent Kitchen Consultants across the United States and abroad. In 2000, about 13 million customers were served driving annual sales that year to over $700 million.

## ▶ PREPARATION FOR SUCCESS

When asked what prepared her to move from her training in education to the role of business owner, Doris reflects on the early years in her career. Upon graduating from college she took a position teaching home economics at a secondary school and found that she loved the experience. After her first year of teaching, a transfer to the Chicago area for her husband's career necessitated that Doris look for related work as the school year had already begun. She landed a position with the University of Illinois Extension Service, a community outreach organization that provided needed agricultural, horticultural, and home economics information to farm and homeowners.

In this position for six years, Doris taught adults many of the same home economics skills that she had shared with her students in the classroom setting. To her delight, adult learners were even more receptive to the information she shared. Extensive public speaking to these adult groups gave Doris key experience and confidence in sharing her ideas. When The Pampered Chef took off, these communication and presentation skills proved to be effective in presenting the products and recruiting Kitchen Consultants to the company.

Doris learned business basics as the company grew. Her husband, an experienced businessman, also proved to be a great source of information and advice. While he always appreciated that this was Doris's company, he offered her support and experience whenever she needed the help. By her own account, Jay and their daughters were her earliest and strongest supporters. At one point, when the company began to experience more rapid growth, he worked for a time in The Pampered Chef business. His specialization was finance, operations and accounting; Doris kept her focus on product selection, marketing and sales. Once the growth spurt was handled and key management positions were in place, Jay returned to his own career work. Today, he provides counsel to the company and is on its Board of Directors.

### ▶ CUTTING EDGE PRODUCTS

All the great ideas in the world would not create a business if the products were not high quality, according to Doris' experience with The Pampered Chef which bills itself as "The Kitchen Store That Comes To Your Door". All of the 175 products in the line are designed to make cooking easier and faster so that customers can spend less time in the kitchen and more time with family and friends. Of particular note are exclusive knives, peelers, shredders, choppers and corers. Serving accessories, measuring tools, baking utensils and cookware are presented along with an extensive line of stoneware. including: pizza stones, bakers, pie plates and bowls.

Seventy-five percent of the company's products are exclusive to The Pampered Chef. Many product innovations take more than a year to develop. Doris remarks that sometimes there is an interest in making a product "cheaper". Instead, her company has taken the position of making products "better by improving them and still offering them at competitive prices." Value-added recipes are packaged along with the products to "pamper" customers with this added benefit.

## ▶ ACCOLADES AND ADVICE

The pampering has surely worked if the awards and achievements Doris and her company have received are any indication. Recognition in *Success, Executive Female, Parents, Working Woman, Fine Cooking* and others over the years has kept the spotlight on the tremendous success of this enterprise founded by a woman with a commitment to balance in her life. In 1994, Ernst & Young, *Inc.* magazine, and Merrill Lynch selected Doris Christopher as the regional winner of the National Entrepreneur of the Year Award in the Masters category. A prestigious ranking in the most recent *Working Woman* magazine has followed subsequent recognition for the company's creative philanthropy to benefit The American Cancer Society and America's Second Harvest. The Pampered Chef achieved the Number 24 spot based on revenue in the publication's annual listing of the Top 500 woman-owned businesses in 2000.

In 1999, Doris wrote a book, *Come to the Table*, published by Warner Books, to share her business story and life philosophy. In it, she celebrates the tradition of family mealtime, honors its deep and lasting roots and reinforces its power to positively impact family life. Some of Doris' thoughts on the subject of mealtime follow here.

- *People yearn to cook.*
- *I believe when families share a meal, the bonds that hold them together grow stronger.*

- *Nourishment is more than the five food groups. At a family meal, there is also nourishment of self-image and worth.*
- *When we listen to others and express our own thoughts we gain understanding, trust, love and commitment.*

In counseling other women on their career decisions, Doris has these thoughts to share.

- *Not everything will be easy. There may be obstacles, but follow your passion.*
- *Be persistent and find work that you totally believe in.*
- *Keep your expenses to a minimum, particularly starting out.*
- *If you are tired, focus on your vision for new energy.*

Doris' vision clearly kept her on the path to The Pampered Chef success. For the first five years she did not draw a salary, choosing to reinvest that money into needed growth. Today, over 20 years later, her steady pursuit of a goal has paid dividends. Daughter, Julie, currently works in the company as a corporate spokesperson. Daughter, Kelley, is an elementary school teacher in suburban Chicago. Even now that the children have grown and have homes of their own, family meals are still a frequent happening at the Christopher's. Through it all, family mealtime continues to matter.

*"Do it anyway."*

**Gwen Willhite**

# Cookie Bouquet/ Cookies by Design

It was the perfect "happily ever after" story: Homecoming Queen marries Football Team Captain and lives happily ever after. Funny thing was, it didn't turn out quite like the original story line.

Mary Gwen Keck grew up in Berryville, Arkansas, watching her grandfather farm the land and build houses to support his family. Her mother ran a local beauty shop. Gwen, who had been the Berryville High School Homecoming Queen, had a promising future when at aged 17 she married the Captain of the football team, Jack Willhite, in 1958 and began what looked like a happy, albeit predictable adult life. Never in her wildest dreams at that time did she think that she would one day create and run a $60 million business that would operate throughout the United States through its franchise network.

Gwen was a headstrong, attractive young woman. While her marriage to Jack eventually ended, she was blessed with the birth of her daughter, Lisa, and remained on good terms with her former husband. Years passed and at age 42, Gwen found herself working in a sheet metal company in Tulsa, Oklahoma as a buyer. It was good work. She had been with this company for 12 years and she liked the job. However, in September of 1983, the company business took a downturn and laid off many of its employees until orders picked up. Gwen was among the chosen and received her first and only pink slip and layoff. She was encouraged by the company to enjoy a few months off, since they would probably be calling her back to work soon. By December, when the phone call did not come to return to work, Gwen had her own wake up call. She was a single parent mom with a 16-year old daughter. She really needed to work.

The Keck family was big on entrepreneurs. Her mother owned a beauty shop. Her grandparents were independent farmers and her grandmother did much of the hands-on work due to her husband's bouts of arthritis. No matter how big or how small the business, the Kecks thought it was better to work for yourself than for somebody else. Gwen could clearly see the logic in this philosophy as she thought about her next career step. She decided to start a business of her own.

The type of business Gwen would run was still a mystery to her. She knew she was "artsy-craftsy" and had creative talent. She went to craft shows looking for ideas and tried her hand at making stuffed animals and other crafts for sale. The work was time intensive and didn't seem like it had great prospects for generating income. Around that time, Mrs. Fields was in the news as a successful venture selling homestyle cookies in retail stores. By the 1980's, cookie consumption in America had increased to be a $2.5 billion industry. Gwen had an idea.

She had seen a plain style of cookie on a stick at the Tulsa, Oklahoma State Fair quite a few years earlier. It occurred to her that there could be a market for cookies on a stick if she could come up with a recipe that was delicious and a cookie that was unique and fun to eat. She set out trying to develop a formula in her kitchen at home in Catoosa, Oklahoma that would work for such a cookie venture.

It was a lot like a research project. Gwen set to work developing a cookie that was delicious, decorative and could be baked with a stick. She bought a supply of flour, sugar and all the other standard cookie ingredients and started baking. She didn't ask anybody anything, but kept to herself as she experimented, baked, took notes, and started over again. Determined her cookies would taste good, she kept up the trial and error for many weeks until she found the formula she was looking for and developed sugar and cinnamon brown sugar cookies that were the origins of the Cookie Bouquet/Cookies By Design line. Almonds, chocolates and candies were the decorations for her early hand-shaped cookies. Icing and shapes came into play about six months later.

Once the recipes were finalized, Gwen worked on cookie arrangements using baskets and ribbon as a holder for an array of cookies. The early delicacies were well received. People liked them. They started asking Gwen if she could make special shapes and sizes. She gave it a try. There weren't very many commercial cookie cutters available at that time, but Gwen started making circle and heart shaped cookies to keep her customers satisfied. As she became more adept at shaped cookies, Gwen bought round commercial cookie cutters, straightened out the material and reshaped them into bears, daisies and other forms of her own design. Today the cookie line features flavors such as peanut butter, chocolate chip, and oatmeal in shapes that include Disney characters, snowmen, dog bones, tulips, ice cream cones, musical instruments, pumpkins and ghosts.

The next hurdle was her search for an icing recipe. Available icings were easy to use but not delicious or attractive. She wanted to develop icing that would take the vibrant colors she had in mind for her cookie decorations. Trial and error again was followed by success as Gwen landed on an icing recipe that would meet her cookie needs.

While Gwen was in the kitchen cooking up her new business, a local businessman had refurbished a little yellow house in the suburb of Tulsa where she lived, to be rented for commercial space. Six weeks after her first sale, Gwen was ready to move out of her kitchen and expand her operation into a 1,000 square foot shop where the cookies could be baked and sold with 14 basic cookies priced at $20. (Decorated cookies were soon offered at 7 for $20.) Cookie Bouquet opened for retail business just six months after the company had been created. There was also a little coffee shop that was part of her business in the new location, a move Gwen came to regret as customers lingering for coffee and a chat with the owner took much needed time away from the focus of baking and building a company. The rent was $350 per month, a big commitment for a new entrepreneur, who paid the rent with the money earned from cookie sales. This little shop was home to the new business for a year and half until Gwen moved to a new location in Tulsa.

## ▶ HUMBLE BEGINNINGS

Early years were learning years. Gwen experimented with recipes and found that cookies baked with pumpkin pie spice smelled great while baking but were terrible to taste. Business lessons were more painful. People would call Gwen to order cookie bouquets to be sent as gifts. They would promise to send a check to cover the cost. In the early years, Gwen accepted this arrangement until she found that about 30% of these orders never sent the money they owed her. At the time, this was perhaps her biggest mistake as the cookie income paid the rent, the employees and kept the business running. Needless to say, the deferred payment policy changed when the shortfall was discovered.

Early years were exhausting years as well. Long days were common. Gwen did whatever it took to keep the business running including cleaning the shop, purchasing ingredients, baking and then icing cookies, and delivering of cookie bouquets. At one point, she reminisces, she was really pleased to get an order for centerpieces at an upscale Tulsa Valentine's Day benefit luncheon held by the Association for Christians and Jews. Unfortunately, the day before Valentine's Day, she was in an automobile accident in which she was badly bruised and many of the cookies were broken. No time to heal and rest, Gwen worked around the clock to recreate the order and deliver it on time.

At the end of the luncheon, many of the attendees who admired the centerpieces drove immediately to the cookie shop hoping to buy more for their own use. Gwen was totally exhausted and unprepared for the influx. She sadly could not fill any walk-in orders that day other than those already in process. At the same time, one of her delivery people mixed up the deliveries he was assigned. To make up for his errors, Gwen refunded the orders for the day and gave all of her customers free cookies. This was one of the toughest times she remembers keeping the business going. At other times, she recalls sleeping until she was exhausted and getting up in the morning to begin again. She cautions that hard work is needed but doesn't mean anything if people don't want what you have to sell.

Gwen was always a likable person. She was kind and trusting, perhaps sometimes to a fault. People obviously thought the world of her. Gwen's relatives and friends worked for free when the business was just getting started. Her best friend, her cousins, neighbors and others supported the new company and cheered for its continued success. As the years went by, many of Gwen's full-time employees and trusted advisors would come from the ranks of those early friends and family members who were so supportive when the company was just a fledgling hoping to survive. Annetta Boney, one of Gwen's early designers and a friend of her daughter is now a vice president in the company to this day.

## ▶ *A LITTLE COOKIE TO A LOT OF DOUGH*

By 1986, Gwen was convinced that she had a business concept that had great potential. She decided to sell her Tulsa store to a buyer that would send her a monthly royalty fee and enable her to move to Dallas, Texas. There she could try her hand at another location in a new, larger market.

Dallas was a really good move. Annetta moved with Gwen as they worked to set up a new store and gain exposure in the new market. One tactic they used was to give cookie bouquets away to individuals and key decision-makers in the community to get people talking about the new business and ordering cookies as gifts. As luck would have it, Gwen's landlady's sister was a food editor for the *Dallas Morning News* and asked to feature the cookie company. Her by-lined newspaper feature on holiday cookie baskets was a quarter page, full-color story on Cookie Bouquet. The publicity brought in such a flurry of excitement that the company could not fill all the orders that called in. Such was the plight of the small new venture that wasn't really capable of handling a huge influx of business like this.

Bit by bit, the company grew. With each step Gwen struggled to stay ahead of the game, make payroll and look for the next move. Independent and committed, she financed her growth with her credit cards after early attempts at bank financing were fruitless. Her focus was always on her goal of creating a company that would give her financial stability by the time she was 60 years old. (Now that she does not need outside financial backing, Gwen has been awarded a line of credit with a bank. She has little use for it at this time.) The first company brochure they developed was created by Gwen and Annetta and run by a local printer. Looking back, while the early brochures were fairly basic, they did the job of selling Cookie Bouquets.

The move to Dallas continued to open new doors and ideas for Gwen and her company. She decided to explore franchising in response to the many requests she received from interested business people. In 1987, the first full franchise opened in Stuttgart, Arkansas. By the time there were eight franchisees, the company reached one million dollars in sales. Gradually the franchise operation grew to the extent that there are now 230 Cookie Bouquet/Cookies By Design franchises in 43 states and more than 203 cities today. Annual sales in the year 2000 were about $60,000,000 quite an achievement from the original concept.

Learning the ropes of franchising brought bumps in the road for Gwen. After three years of franchising, her business contract was challenged by one of her franchisees. It came to light that her legal advice on the creation of this contract was not appropriate for a large company. Gwen's trusting style had taken the contract at face value. The conflict with this franchisee finally ended fairly amicably. Since then, Gwen has new legal advisors on her team.

Another hurdle appeared in 1990, when the Cookie Bouquet name was challenged in San Jose, California by a business owner who was using the company name, The Cookie Florist, and selling "cookie bouquets". There was enough California common law that Gwen's case for winning was not clear-cut. Her attorney advised her to offer the second name of Cookies By Design, which was easily trademarked, and became a new name choice that franchisees could operate. Gwen was not happy with this outcome, but she lived with it. Years later, she tried again for a copyright and was granted one for the Cookie Bouquet name, since she had established name equity in it by then. Today, the business operates under both banners and describes their product as "cookie arrangements".

While the company has grown in large scale, Gwen maintains a modest headquarters staff of 20 to run the business. Linda Shunk, a former Dallas financial consultant, came on board in 1992 as business manager and helped Gwen grow the company at a rapid pace. Today, Linda serves as president and chief executive officer of the company, since Gwen assumed the role of chairman. Longtime employee and family friend, Katie Patterson and her husband, David, are also key to the management team. The company is focused on serving the franchise operators to help them succeed and grow. They are now based in a 6,000 square foot office space in Dallas, Texas, which houses staff, and Cookie College training operations. (Everyone in the business attends Cookie College to learn the basics of the cookie business.)

A labor-intensive process, all Cookie Bouquet and Cookies By Design arrangements are made fresh in the local franchise shops. Headquarters provides recipes and training. The franchisees are required to purchase patented containers from the parent company. Gwen explains further, *"Getting the cookies on sticks to be displayed in an arrangement was one of the difficult steps for this business. Several years ago, I was able to design and produce a unique and patented container that is manufactured exclusively for our chain. This is an achievement I am very proud of and is a great labor saving device in our business."*

One unusual twist in this franchise group is their policy of referring any cookie orders phoned in for long distance delivery to the nearest operator to the gift recipient. Long distance shipping is not preferred as a means to offer the freshest undamaged arrangement to the final destination. "What goes around comes around" is the motto that supports this approach to referrals among the franchisees.

The full line of Cookie Bouquet/Cookies By Design products can be seen on-line at their websites *www.cookiebouquet.com* and *www.cookiesbydesign.com*. There are also brochures available at most shops that show the product line to walk-in customers.

## ▶ GWEN'S THOUGHTS ON THE PAST AND THE FUTURE

*"I have always had strong, independent women in my family as role models,"* Gwen reflects. *"People in my family didn't work for other people very often. Early on, I learned to do things for myself. I didn't think I had limits. I knew I could do it when I started the business. My family has always believed that hard work is what it takes to succeed."* Her mother is still alive today and just sold her own beauty shop a few years ago.

When asked if it helped or hurt to be a woman in her venture, she answered that bank financing was an issue at times early on, but she learned to live without it. After being denied a loan in her early requests, she decided not to subject herself to the process anymore. On the positive side, Gwen believes it was an asset in a cookie business to have the owner as an image of "mom in the kitchen" baking homemade goodness to eat.

Looking forward, today's challenges to Gwen as chairman and strategic planner for the company, involve keeping the franchise operators serviced and meeting their needs. With a diverse group of operators, the organization constantly works to keep everyone involved and a "member of the family" since each franchisee is so important to the overall company. On an annual basis, the organization brings this group together for conferences to discuss new visions and directions.

Gwen does not plan any major new ventures for herself in the business arena. She still enjoys her work in the cookie business, is proud of what she has accomplished and is now able to enjoy her favorite pastimes as her major business goals have been met just in time for her 60th birthday. An animal lover, she has three dogs on her property. Gwen's home is decorated comfortably with her antiques collected over the years.

In 1999, Gwen took a second residence back in her hometown in the Ozarks area of northwest Arkansas. About the same time, her daughter, Lisa, sold her Cookies By Design franchise in Dallas and moved back to Arkansas with her daughter, Danielle. Another personal milestone Gwen is pleased to be in the midst of is the construction of a large, new second home with extensive landscaping and gardens, located in an area of Arkansas where both of her parents and many relatives still live. (Her father still helps clear the property with a chain saw when needed.) Daughter and granddaughter will be living nearby when the new home construction is completed. Lisa is a great help tending to her mother's property when Gwen is traveling and involved in running the cookie business.

On another personal note, Gwen confides that her real passion in life is flower gardening. She hopes to help a friend who is a company franchisee and certified a landscape designer, with a gardening business in her free time. By recent accounts, Gwen is doing much of the planting of her new home gardens herself. She considers it a labor of love.

In conclusion, Gwen reflects, *"I am still the same person basically as I was when I began Cookie Bouquet back in Tulsa, Oklahoma. I may have a few more things, but my beliefs and values are still the same. I learned a lot along the way, but I have no regrets."* She went on to say, *"The names of the people who were difficult I have forgotten. Those individuals who helped me at each step I will never forget."* Her kindness and her down to earth style, big picture approach, and creative easygoing way in her life and business has kept Gwen Willhite grounded in the midst of enormous success. She defines success as having achieved her goals, having a comfortable life with peace of mind, and the ability to enjoy life.

It's time to enjoy life *now* according to Gwen's lifetime plans.

Her story of persistence and imagination will likely be real food for thought to many women as they go about their tasks in the kitchen in their own homes. *"Do it anyway,"* the motto that has guided her from year to year, is her advice to women who would like to follow their own personal dreams.

Perhaps homemaking guru, Martha Stewart puts Gwen Willhite's work into a new perspective when she remarks, "I think baking cookies is equal to Queen Victoria running a kingdom."

For Gwen Willhite, perhaps it is.

> *"You can't celebrate on the mountain tops if you haven't been in the valleys."*
>
> **Arlene Lenarz**

# Mary Kay Cosmetics

Arlene Lenarz has earned approximately $65,000 a month in commissions this year selling Mary Kay, products. As the number one Independent Executive National Sales Director, Arlene approximates annual earnings of around $800,000 as recently reported in *Applause* magazine published for Mary Kay Independent Beauty Consultants. In fact, in her

28th year with the company, Arlene has achieved total Mary Kay career earnings in excess of $8 million. Incidentally, she worked from her home the entire time.

Poised, elegant and inspiring are the words her business associates called to mind when asked about Arlene. The beauty and polish of a homecoming queen are her exterior qualities from which personal enthusiasm and wisdom pour forth. The energy and full attention to anyone she is with make others feel special and more powerful in her presence. Meticulously and professionally dressed, her careful attention to detail underscores her success as a motivator, a mentor and a business professional among the highest ranks of the independent Mary Kay sales force organization today.

How did a stay-at-home mom with four children who had retired from nursing to spend ten years as a professional homemaker find herself as a Mary Kay superstar? It was an August day in 1972 when Arlene took a break from watching her regular soap opera on television to answer a telephone call from an enthusiastic Mary Kay Beauty Consultant. The caller offered a complimentary facial and makeover for Arlene and some of her friends. It sounded like fun, so they made arrangements for a session the following Friday.

At this point in her life, Arlene claimed that she had long ago mastered the art of housekeeping. Her children were healthy and grown, ranging in ages from six to 12 years old. While she did not want to return to the hectic schedule of her nursing career, she yearned for something more in her daily life. Her husband, Dick, provided very well for the family's needs, but she was aware that the college years were around the corner for her children. Financing college tuition for her four children would be challenging.

With these thoughts in mind, Arlene was very interested in the skin care class she had scheduled. She wondered about the work of the Mary Kay Independent Beauty Consultants. What did they do exactly to sell cosmetics? What was the allure of a cosmetic program like this one?

Arlene was blessed with the type of all-American good looks that exude a natural beauty. She personally had never had a complete skin care program and was curious about the line she was about to experience. As she watched the Mary Kay Consultant work with such enjoyment and enthusiasm demonstrating cosmetic makeovers for her women guests, Arlene wondered if this was something that she could do? The Independent Beauty Consultant confided that she was having fun, that the product sold itself and that she was making full-time pay on part-time hours. The skin care class was a big hit with everyone who attended.

After the class, the Consultant invited Arlene to a Mary Kay coffee to meet her Independent Sales Director the following Monday. Arlene agreed to attend. When she shared her plans with close friends and her mother, she was discouraged by their reactions. At the time, Arlene was painfully shy in group settings and had never sold anything, not even a Girl Scout cookie. They told her to consider nursing again and forget about Mary Kay. When Arlene called her Consultant contact to share these concerns the Consultant asked, "When are you going to stop letting other people tell you how to live your life?" Putting her fears aside, Arlene attended the meeting. Positive ideas, new products, great marketing and personal support and encouragement surrounded her. By her account, that day her life was turned around and she became a Mary Kay Independent Beauty Consultant.

Eager to share her big news, Arlene hurried home to tell her husband, Dick, about her new career. His reaction was reserved. He asked, "Are you in Mary Kay for something to do or are you in Mary Kay to do something?" While they had always dreamed of owning a business together, Dick did not share Arlene's vision for this venture at the outset. Still, he helped her carry her supplies into the house and watched her progress with Mary Kay in the early weeks. Bit by bit, he got more interested and was soon fully supportive of Arlene's work. "When I asked him to help me with the bookkeeping for my incoming orders, Dick finally realized that my Mary Kay business had huge potential and I was determined to make it a big success," Arlene reflects.

Arlene was passionate about her Mary Kay business. Some days were challenging early on as she grew into the position. Nevertheless, she loved every day of it. *"If you love what you do, you will never work another day in your life,"* she explains. The company did and still does live by the Golden Rule statement of priorities, *"Take care of your faith, family, and career,"* in that order. This is in keeping with Arlene's personal life philosophy today.

After one year, Arlene had created Lenarz Leaders, a sales unit of 41 new Beauty Consultants. Her vision and enthusiasm were contagious. In two years, Arlene's Mary Kay income surpassed Dick's salary at the time. The work that she had begun for college savings, school shoes and clothes had become a greater success than she had ever imagined. That same year, the Lenarz sales unit earned the use of a coveted pink Cadillac, awarded as a mark of distinction to the unit leader, an honor she continues to enjoy today. That same year, the unit was in the top 10 in the world of Mary Kay.

Year after year, Lenarz Leaders won high honors for their sales achievements. In 1977, they were the #1 unit in all of Mary Kay's sales force organization. By 1978, they had reached $1 million in sales. Today, her area includes over 5,000 Independent Beauty Consultants and a team of 175 Independent Sales Directors in the United States, Canada, Mexico, and the Philippines.

Arlene's enthusiasm, positive attitude, team spirit, persistence, and concern for others are the foundation of her success. Another Consultant remarks, "Arlene is a people-builder; she motivates everyone to really be all they can be." Numerous Mary Kay annual awards for leadership have been earned by Arlene including the Go-Give Award, Millionaires Club, President's Circle, Inner Circle, Executive National Sales Director and for the past five years she has earned the ranking as the Number One National Sales Director for Mary Kay.

Arlene's career commitment is a perfect match for the Mary Kay opportunity. The company was founded in 1963 by Mary Kay Ash, an accomplished sales professional, who recognized a need for more women's positions in the male-dominated business world. Her goal was, "to provide women with an unlimited opportunity for personal and financial success." Her approach, praise your sales team to success. Positive reinforcement, encouragement, education, and recognition are the tools she used to help her people and her sales grow. Spectacular annual meetings and lavish award programs keep team goals in focus. From its home-based origins, the skin products company has thrived and for many years has been one of the best-selling brands of color cosmetics and facial skin care products in the United States.

Accolades for the company are too numerous to include them all, but *Fortune* magazine recognized it as one of "The 100 Best Companies to Work for in America," and one of the "10 Best Companies for Women." The company now includes approximately 750,000 independent beauty consultants in 37 countries worldwide. In 2000, estimated wholesale sales were more than $1.2billion, which equates to more than $2.4billion at the retail level. The company's primary goal, as stated in its mission statement is to enrich women's lives.

## ▶ ARLENE'S THOUGHTS

What were some of the thoughts and approaches Arlene used to drive her success?

- *Some days are not easy and only your personal discipline keeps you going.*
- *You can't celebrate on the mountain tops if you haven't been in the valleys.*
- *A mistake or failure is an event. Leave the experience and take the lesson.*
- *Success is a daily progression toward a worthwhile goal.*
- *We are not born winners or born losers. We are all born choosers.*
- *Your success is hidden in your daily routine.*
- *Plan your success. A goal without a written plan is only a wish.*
- *Law of the Universe: the giver is the receiver.*
- *Find life work you love and believe in.*
- *Believe in yourself.*

Arlene lives her philosophy. She is passionate about her work and her family. Several years after her Mary Kay business became successful, her husband retired early from his job. His support with the family, community interests, and her career has been of great help. In November 1999, her daughter, Gayle, became a Mary Kay Sales Director and has since earned the pink Cadillac achievement. Her daughter, Karin, a Mary Kay Beauty Consultant, just earned the use of a Pontiac Grand Am.

Her heroes in life are Mary Kay Ash and her own mother, Helen, who was a working mom when Arlene was a child. The work ethic and positive attitudes learned from these women inspire Arlene to even greater accomplishments as a leader in the Mary Kay sales force organization, as a wife, mother, and grandmother of five.

It is interesting to note this Millionaire Woman still works from home. The family has moved three times since Arlene joined Mary Kay. Their current home in Eden Prairie, Minnesota is 7,000 square feet. It includes ample workspace for Arlene and a separate office for her assistant, computer, and files. As she enjoys her cherry paneled office and beautiful décor, she reflects, *"Mary Kay is really all about women helping women . . . to feel beautiful, to be empowered, to grow. The product and the process are a great combination for success."*

*"Look for Learning Moments in whatever you do."*

**Lane Nemeth**

# Discovery Toys

Who is Lane Nemeth, the founder of Discovery Toys? How did an English major from the University of Pittsburgh end up creating and running one of the largest companies to sell educational toys in the United States? Was it her outspoken style or her insistence on leading life her own way, balancing a career and a family at the same time, that lead her to this business

53

success story? In 1977, Discovery Toys was created as an outgrowth of Lane Nemeth's personal mission statement. A tale of persistence in the face of great challenge, here is her story.

When Lane Nemeth was trying to decide what field to study in college, business wasn't even a consideration. Women students were preparing themselves to be teachers, social workers, nurses or home economists. There were few, if any, coeds in the business school at the University of Pittsburgh, her alma mater, when Lane was in college.

Lane decided to pursue a Bachelor of Arts degree in English literature. While she wasn't sure if it was part of her life calling, it seemed like a good thing to do at the time. Shortly after, she went on to complete a master's degree in education from Seton Hall University. Little did she know that one day in the near future, she would create an educational toy company that would reach $100 million in annual revenue.

After graduation, Lane and her husband, Ed, were newlyweds living in South Orange, New Jersey, near the town where they were raised. Ed had been accepted into the master's program to study physics at the University of Oregon in Eugene. The couple saw the move as an adventure and decided to make the big move out west.

Lane was excited to begin working in education now that her formal training was completed. However, in the early 1970's there was an overabundance of teachers trained for a limited number of openings. In short, like so many other fresh graduates, she could not find a teaching job. She ended up finding work in a day care center for $1.50 an hour wages. By then, Lane had to do something, actually anything, to generate income while Ed was in school. Low wages were better than no wages.

Times were tough. They were living in low-cost student housing, but Lane's paycheck did not go very far. For a while, they had to apply for food stamps just to survive.

In frustration, Lane gave up her search for a "real" teaching job, took the civil-service exam and landed a job working for the state welfare department, checking on welfare patients in nursing homes, a sad and difficult assignment. Over time, she moved up in the state system and was promoted to a position with management and public speaking responsibilities, work that she came to enjoy.

Meanwhile, Ed completed his master's degree in physics. Jobs in his field were not available in Eugene, so they decided to move again. This time, they relocated to San Francisco, California at a time when Lane's parents had planned to move there also. Once again, Lane found there were no schoolteacher openings and ended up working in day care. This time, she found a position as director of the Concord ChildCare Center. Lane really enjoyed working with preschoolers and managing her staff. Although she trained for a more formal educational setting, she totally enjoyed the preschoolers. It gave her great satisfaction and a sense of accomplishment to help the young parents with their questions and concerns about each child's educational development.

In October 1975, Lane and Ed became new parents themselves with the birth of their daughter, Tara, whom they adored. Even at the peak of their excitement though, things were changing in their lives. Lane did not want to leave Tara and return to work full-time. After six months as a "stay-at-home mom", she ultimately decided to work part-time. Ed was working in a startup company so the extra income was needed. Likewise, Lane had to admit that she enjoyed the mental stimulation and achievement she felt from her career. The compromise of her part-time employment seemed to be the best solution to their dilemma.

For one year, Lane worked on a flexible schedule for her former employer, the Concord ChildCare Center. At times, she felt physically and emotionally torn by her longing to be with Tara and her interest or need for her own work. This is an inner struggle she found many young mothers deal with on a day-to-day basis. Lane reached a breaking point with this tension over a policy she encountered at work.

As director of the day care center, she was thrilled to have access to creative, educational toys that the state-owned center bought through specialty catalogues. Lane believed these were terrific toys for Tara. But this type of valuable, attractive toy was not available in retail stores. Lane decided to prepare a small order for her personal purchase and inquired as to how she should pay for it. That's when bureaucracy stepped in. Lane's order was blocked. She was told that only institutions could buy these toys, according to state policy. That was it. Lane had had enough.

By then, she was fed up with the bureaucratic policies at her work. She was tired of the strain of working for someone else while trying to take first-rate care of Tara. By personality, Lane preferred not to have a boss, but to be the boss, since she never enjoyed working for someone else. So, she quit. She was sure there was a better way to raise her child and run her life. In fact, she already had some ideas on how to do this.

The lack of great creative toys for children in the general retail market was the reason Lane was so excited and driven to buy toys from the institutional market. If she was having trouble finding these toys, other parents must be having the same challenge.

Adversity can be the spark to set off a great new idea. Lane's frustration lead her to think of a business opportunity she could see in delivering educational toys to eager parents and children. Her first idea was to open a toy store and hold seminars for parents on how to raise bright, happy children. Her master's degree in education, her work experience in day care and her consumer frustration uniquely qualified Lane to create such a business. She asked her husband and her father, who was a marketing professional, what they thought of the concept.

Lane's dad liked the idea, but thought the delivery system was limited. He questioned how many parents were looking for classes like she proposed? Would one retail location be able to compete with the big chain toy stores? Ed listened and came up with another idea. He suggested Lane sell toys using a distribution approach that Tupperware used so effectively, home sales.

The idea sounded like a winner to Lane. Her experience, passion, love of motherhood and work could all fit into this new equation. That day in 1977, Discovery Toys was born.

## ▶ THE REAL WORK HAD JUST BEGUN

At this point, Lane realized she was really low on career business experience, limited only to short-term job experiences as a young woman. Nevertheless, what she lacked in formal business training, she made up for in passion for the Discovery Toys' work. She knew that a flexible career would give her prime time with Tara and the best of both worlds. Using her home as her base and $5000 she borrowed from her grandmother, Elizabeth Perlowing, Lane set about researching commercially available toys that were attractive, sturdy, and most important, educational. The first step was a trip to a toy trade show in Los Angeles, California at the Biltmore Hotel.

Towers of boxes in bright colors were everywhere. But close inspection uncovered that toy after toy was poorly made, in a flashy package, but with little or no real educational value. It looked as if the toy business was really all about packaging versus product value.

Tired and discouraged, Lane and her friend, Sue Nurock, stumbled into one of the last trade show booths they were to visit. It was Richard Bendett's toy booth. Finally, here were the items they were hoping to find. Lane and Sue began opening packages and testing toys right on the floor of the booth. Toys and boxes were everywhere. A dazed, but pleased Richard ended the show with Lane's first Discovery Toy order.

When the shipment arrived, boxes again were everywhere, this time in Lane's garage, kitchen and bedroom. Although Lane scheduled home demonstrations immediately, it was clear they were going to need salespeople as soon as possible to make room in their home for a life.

Lane ran the ad in the local newspaper. The classified advertisement read: "Schoolteachers Wanted to Sell Educational Toys and Games." She had a hunch that teachers would love the idea of selling educational toys. It was a good hunch. As people responded to the ad, the ranks grew of "educational consultants", the position title of Discovery Toys' sales representatives.

Business was brisk with a demonstration schedule filling up. But a problem was developing because cash was not collected at the time of the order. Lane's father urged her to "get the money up front" so she would not run out of capital for the company.

"Cash flow" was a new concept to Lane, but she was learning fast. She claims this advice from her dad saved her business.

One year into the venture, they had sold $20,000 of Discovery toys and knew it was time to rent additional space. It wasn't easy. Landlords had no interest in a woman tenant. Finally, Lane found a small, 900 square foot, run-down space without heat, light or much paint on the walls in Concord, California. She was able to rent this office/warehouse space only after Ed agreed to co-sign the lease.

One hurdle crossed, another seemed to continually appear. In January 1978, after Discovery Toys had incorporated, Lane visited with her banker to secure a loan for needed funding. "Sorry, not interested," was the response the fledgling company heard at bank after bank. Money was sorely needed for rent, inventory and commissions. Lane was once again in a real bind.

Luck and family answered her call for help. Lane's brother-in-law, Walt Weissman, believed in the new company's promise and loaned it $50,000. New debt added new pressure but it also forced Lane to keep looking for ideas for new growth potential. Product lines eventually expanded to include toys, games, books and software.

In 1978, there were 40 educational consultants working for the toy company. By October of that year they had sold $100,000 in orders with the two largest sales months of the year coming up fast. It was good news, bad news. They had oversold their inventory and could not get product fast enough. Letters of apology, refunds, deliveries of complimentary products were the embarrassing routine until systems and fulfillment could be corrected.

When asked if she ever "hit the wall" running the business Lane candidly shares, *"About every six months I would find myself exhausted by the new challenges that kept coming up."* And so it went. Finance, staffing, inventory, facility, product design and distribution challenges were met and resolved every step of the way. With each step of growth came new considerations. Lane met them all head-on with determination and commitment. The mission of Discovery Toys carried her through many difficult times. That mission was:

1. *To encourage children and families to grow through play, and*
2. *To offer women attractive work opportunity that allows flexible schedules to work around children's needs and schedules. (Successful educational consultants' earnings range from $30,000 to mid six figures plus, per year.)*

Year by year, Discovery Toys continued its steady growth. Lane is convinced that true business and personal success are only possible if you believe in what you do. Your personal mission statement or life philosophy has to be compatible with the mission of your company. Lane's personal life goals and values are woven into the fabric of the work and purpose of her toy company. Over the years, she has been able to blend her career work with a commitment to "mommy and Tara time" when they would spend hours together enjoying one another and playing with the toys her mother had designed or was distributing. Tara, now a young woman, still likes to have time one-on-one to visit with her mother.

Business challenges came and went as the company continued through the years. Personal challenges were, of course, part of the mix too. In 1979, Lane was in a serious automobile accident. She fortunately recovered quickly.

The ups and downs of child rearing were her personal priority. Lane's business travel that was needed to buy inventory and manage the business always required an adjustment day for Tara. Role expectations and pressures on her relationship with Ed had to be talked out between them. He has admitted that it can be challenging to be the spouse of an entrepreneur.

Experiences with her staff brought highs and lows into the Discovery Toy chronicles. The impact of managers, whether ineffective or a terrific asset, was definitely part of Lane's story. Perhaps the saddest story of Lane's Discovery Toy years was the death of the company's chief operating officer in 1992. Mike Clark was a great leader for the management team and a source of support for Lane in the company's operation. After his death, it required even more energy for Lane to carry on with the challenges of the business without his enthusiasm and support of the team.

Lane was used to hard work and persistence. While the experience was never quite the same, she carried on and worked harder to fulfill her promises to her staff and her customers. Discovery Toys had become one of the leading direct sellers of educational toys, games, books and software by that time, doing business in the United States and Canada. Its headquarters were eventually housed in Livermore, California in an 180,000 square foot building that included its corporate offices, distribution and service centers. About 35,000 educational consultants were selling Discovery Toys. Over 100 people were on board as headquarters staff.

## ▶ TIME TO MOVE ON

In 1997, after 20 years of creating, running and building Discovery Toys, Lane Nemeth decided it was time to move on with her life. She was tired beyond her imagination and felt like she was literally carrying the weight of the company for 20 years. Avon Products offered to buy the business and Lane was ready to sell. She has remained involved with the company in a consultant capacity. Since the sale to Avon, the company has been resold to a small private company.

Along the way, Lane has earned numerous awards and has written a book about her philosophies of life, child rearing, business and educational toys. The book, *Discovering Another Way,* details Lane's life story and beliefs while it shares thoughtful "learning moments" with the reader. She still gets letters from parents thanking her for helping them raise "phenomenal kids". While her heart and interest continue on with Discovery Toys, Lane is already up and running with another new venture.

Lane took time out for a few months of rest and relaxation following the sale of the toy company. Her creative mind kept moving while her body took a break. In less than a year, she had an idea for a new business. "One Day MBA", Lane's new company, offers individuals and companies a curriculum of seminars, course work, and coaching in strategic planning, business planning, technology, sales, and marketing. Full details of this exciting new venture can be found at the company website, www.onedaymba.com. Although the business is in its early stages, it will certainly be a company to watch with Lane's experience, creativity and persistence.

Looking back, Lane reflects, *"Relationships are everything in life and in business; women are really better than most men at building ties like this."* She comments that while it was hard in some ways being a woman in business at a time when so few women were heading companies, her gender was an asset in the choice of business she created. She went on to add that her business really grew out of her commitment to building a strong relationship with her daughter and her husband. In this light, the business was an outgrowth of her life mission and key relationships.

Her advice to other women entrepreneurs: *"If you are driven to start a company, decide your goals and know that it can be a 60 to 80 hour work week. It may require ridiculous hours and commitment. But when all is said and done, it won't matter if you have a lot of money and your relationships are a mess. Whatever you do, don't give up your family."*

Lane and Ed are still together. Through the years, Ed has been Lane's greatest support. She admits that Discovery Toys could never have prospered without Ed's constant encouragement and help. Today, the Nemeths still tremendously enjoy their daughter, Tara, who is now in her mid 20's and planning an advanced degree in child psychology. While Lane may be on to a new business discovery, her personal mission statement to help others and lead a balanced life goes with her into the next new venture.

# Success Secrets

## CLUSTER ONE—
## Getting Started

**S**ixteen women with sixteen stories of business success have shared their wisdom and the highlights of their journey. There were no roadmaps to follow on the path to their individual achievement. In fact, their unique approach to their goals was the very foundation of their ultimate accomplishment. There are, however, a number of common themes and approaches in each of these unique profiles. These winning approaches are the Success Secrets this group of women were willing to share with us to offer their experience as guidelines for others' future success.

It would be impossible to capture the total wisdom and counsel of these sixteen Millionaire Women, but their most powerful messages will follow here.

### ▶ SUCCESS SECRET #1: Start with Yourself

Knowledge of your own strengths, weaknesses and opportunities is critical to your ultimate success. What motivates you? What are your needs and wants? What do you believe are your strongest capabilities? What experience can you bring to a new endeavor? What ideas can you generate that will launch a new venture? What assets and allies do you have to sustain your work? This introspection is the most critical piece of work an individual must undertake to focus on an entrepreneurial or career direction.

While all of the women profiled in this book made reference to this step in one way or another, Doris Christopher speaks directly about her search to combine her personal and career expertise with a business idea that would work well with her family values and schedule, and offer a valuable benefit to other women. Pampered Chef came to be after much introspection on Doris' part about making the most of her home economics and personal communication skills to meet an existing market need. Likewise, Lane Nemeth realized that she had developed an expertise in early childhood education that gave her insights into what educational toys would be of value in an everyday at-home play experience for children. Arlene Lenarz identified with the Mary Kay Cosmetics consultant that presented to her guests at a home party. Arlene thought this was a work experience that she would find enjoyable and rewarding. With the success and growth of Mrs. Fields Cookies in the news coast-to-coast, Cookie Bouquet founder, Gwen Willhite, realized that the home-baked cookies business had become a growing industry that she was well qualified and enthusiastic about joining.

It may be possible to succeed without an understanding of who you are and what motivation, ability and ideas are your strengths. However, this first step increases the odds of sustained success by a wide margin.

Some people seem to spend more time on introspection by nature. Many have developed a good sense of who they are as an individual and what their personal strengths, preferences and weaknesses are. For anyone who would like to pursue more self-knowledge of this kind, there are many resources to turn to now. Career counselors, career coaches, psychologists and human resource professionals provide such services using a range of testing and evaluative instruments as well as personal counseling. The public library and the Internet are the most broad-based information sources for books and self-assessment tools. A reference librarian would be of great assistance locating the latest and most reliable books available on this subject.

For specific self-evaluation, several instruments are widely recognized and used by university placement offices as well as professional career counselors. These are the Myers-Briggs Type Inventory and the Keirsey Temperment Sorter, two surveys that identify a person's basic personality and temperment type and relate it to potentially satisfying career choices. By sorting an individual's answers to a series of pertinent questions, these tools offer input on personal and career strengths and preferences. An online search using either of these test names will uncover a path to practical Internet opportunities to use these instruments conveniently from home. A Department of Labor website (www.dol.gov) offers job satisfaction reports matching categories of work for each of the 16 basic personality/temperament types. The Keirsey Temperament Sorter is also available in the books *Please Understand Me* and *Please Understand Me Part II*, written by David Keirsey. These can be found in most public libraries.

## ▶ *SUCCESS SECRET #2: Find a Need and Fill It*

"Find a need and fill it," sounds so simple, but it works. The Millionaire Women all spent time observing, thinking and talking with people about what the needs and wants of their potential purchasers were. It is this thoughtful, observant approach that offers valuable input for analysis as to whether the goods or services a new entrepreneur would like to offer would have any significant demand for them.

Lane Nemeth of Discovery Toys knew from her own experiences that educational toys were difficult to purchase for parents who were looking for alternatives to retail toy store selections. Doris Christopher of Pampered Chef watched the trend of working mothers rising and saw that she could improve the quality and efficiency of their time in the kitchen. Gwen

Willhite of Cookie Bouquet kept in touch with the national and local news around her. It was apparent to her that the public was eagerly embracing the opportunity to purchase home-baked quality cookies for eating or sharing as gifts. It was clear to Arlene Lenarz that there was a proven demand for Mary Kay Cosmetics. Her goal was to create a business of her own that would grow alongside the growth of the cosmetics leader as it gained market penetration and branched out into new countries. These are but a few of the examples of this principle in action: Find a want or a need that is going unfilled or could be delivered at a higher quality or a lower price, and then find a way to fill that niche.

The process of "need identification" will include both product and market strategic assessment. Formal research may be a step that a new entrepreneur will want to consider. Hiring a research firm is an option that will require its own homework to ensure that the source used is reputable and capable in the area and scope of the given project. Ample research sources are already available through industry publications, library reference materials, and government reports on a vast range of industry and market segments.

*The Occupational Outlook Handbook,* available through the U.S. Bureau of Labor Statistics at www.bls.gov, is one government publication that lists job descriptions, salary ranges and the availability of positions in various industries now and in the future. A source such as this may substantiate a hunch about a given sector of the economy's projected growth and the market's demand for that service or product.

In conclusion, it may not be essential that a brand new "need" be identified to launch a successful new business. There may exist options that could be improved by 5% to 50% in performance, price or availability. Amazon.com is the perfect example of a new distribution channel for the purchase of books. The concept of buying books was not new. It was the method of distribution that spoke to society's wants and needs for timesaving options in making purchases.

It is always a good idea to find the customer you are considering selling to and question a few of them about whether they think your product or service idea would meet their need and at what price would it be of value to them. Research firms can also help with this step through focus groups and random testing.

## ▶ *SUCCESS SECRET #3:*
## *Dream, Imagine, Challenge Yourself*

Every one of the women profiled in this book allowed herself to dream, to think big, to imagine a product or service that was not available yet to their customers. At times, the process was challenging, confusing, unnerving and daunting. Other times, the time spent dreaming, investigating, creating plans and setting goals was exhilarating. With or without the support of those closest to them, the Millionaire Women allowed their imagination to take them to the realm of possibilities beyond the realities of the present.

Ideas were considered and discarded for a variety of reasons. Gwen Willhite's initial teddy bear craft experiment was cast aside in favor of a cookie company. Lane Nemeth's initial toyshop idea was discarded for a broader product distribution through catalogue and home sales. Arlene Lenarz disregarded the skepticism of those who pointed out her lack of business experience when she began and focused on her goals and dreams of success. Through it all, the dream, the vision of these entrepreneurs carried them forward.

Some had an end goal that inspired them to start a business that would yield financial rewards. An independent work schedule and experience, college tuition, significant income without limits, vacation homes were all among the goals shared by The Millionaire Women. Some had a specific product that was the inspiration for a new business. Others sought success and looked for the venue that would allow them to achieve it.

Throughout their experience, all of these successful women had a vision, a dream of what was possible in a new business and what the positive consequences could be for their lives. No one gave them permission to "think out of the box". They just did it with an understanding that you cannot move to a new level of success if you can't imagine where you are going first.

There are countless books written on the subject of goals, dreams and vision, many of which are well-worth reading to explore the power of this aspect of success. In fact, there are entire companies that deliver the information and tools needed to encourage creativity, vision and goal setting for individuals and organizations. Nightingale-Conant (www.nightingale.com) and Successories (www.successories.com) are two widely known businesses in this field.

One of the great foundation books on this subject is *Think & Grow Rich* by Napolean Hill (1960 revised edition) who shares the secret he learned from Andrew Carnegie, one of the early millionaires in the United States. While the book explores the secret in great detail its premise is that "thoughts are things" and that we move in the direction of our predominant thought. In fact, the power of vision, the phenomenon explored in Hill's book, has been a core component of the success profiles featured here and a Success Secret of today's Millionaire Women.

## ▶ SUCCESS SECRET #4:
### Find and Follow Your Passion

This Success Secret is deeply rooted in self-knowledge, but in a very particular way. "Passion" is a buzzword today used by many. In the context of venturing into an ambitious pursuit, it is essential to discover, what activities or experiences you have in which you are totally involved and present to the moment? What times were you experiencing something and time flew by so that several hours felt like just a few minutes had passed? Identifying your passion involves finding out what you really enjoy doing in your life.

Yet, it implies even more commitment to the interest. It is the intensity of the interest or enjoyment that sets a "passion" apart. Sports celebrities, famous writers, politicians are among the first that come to mind when looking for examples of people with a passion for their work. The sixteen women featured here all possess passion for their work and their success.

People who are passionate about their life, their work, an ideal, or a belief are all around us in everyday life if we take the time to find them. Everyone is not "passionate" about something, but there are many individual who are. Observe these persons and the manifestations of passion and its power will become obvious.

Arlene Lenarz of Mary Kay Cosmetics shares that if you find your passion in your career, you will never work another day in your life, because your days will be spent doing something you enjoy. Those people who truly follow their passion through ups and downs realize that the work may be hard but it can be exhilarating and a force driving that person to ultimate success.

"Spend
wisely and
have a
business
plan."

Lillian
Vernon

# Lillian Vernon
# Corporation

Lillian Menasche was a happy child in a prosperous, well-established family in Leipzig, Germany. Her early childhood memories linger on her beautiful mother, her intelligent and sophisticated father, her loving older brother, Fred, and their comfortable upper class life in a brick villa on a treelined street in Leipzig. Until the winter of 1932, it was a picture perfect childhood remembered for frequent skating parties and bonfires with friends on the frozen pond on the property.

Lillian's father, Herman, with his wife, Erna's help, had worked hard and grown prosperous in the lingerie trade. In January of 1933, Adolph Hitler became chancellor of Germany, which put German Jews there in danger. Frequent shouts of "Heil Hitler" were heard. Lillian and Fred were often taunted as they walked to school. Within months, the ultimate blow came. Nazi soldiers arrived at the Menasche home, unannounced, one day and ordered the family to leave. The family watched in frustration and sadness as the soldiers turned their home into Nazi headquarters.

Upheaval and change became a way of life as Herman and Erna moved the family to Amsterdam in the Netherlands, and later, to Palestine (now Israel) and finally, to New York City to avoid danger.

Language barriers and a new culture brought many lonely times for Lillian while growing up. Her father's optimism and determination as an entrepreneur were traits she admired and hoped to follow. Family discussions during dinner of Herman's apparel and then, small leather goods manufacturing businesses nurtured her knowledge and curiosity for the world of business. Her part time jobs as a sales clerk in a Barton's candy store and as an usherette at the Riverside Movie Theater taught her about retailing and improved her fluency in the English language. As a teenager, her father asked her to create designs of purses. Her creations all sold well and she realized that she had an "eye for winners" and a "golden gut" for what people needed and wanted to buy.

In 1949, Lillian met and married Sam Hochberg, after a whirlwind courtship topped off by a lavish wedding at the Astor Hotel on Broadway in New York City. As newlyweds, Sam worked in his family's dry goods store, while Lillian set up their apartment in Mount Vernon, a pleasant suburb of New York City. Once their new home was in order, she fine-tuned her daily household chores to only twelve minutes and worked part-time as a bookkeeper and as a retail sales clerk to earn money for the "extras that made life fun."

Two years later while expecting her first child, Lillian knew they would need a larger apartment and more income. In those days, women rarely worked outside the home and a pregnant woman who worked was considered an embarrassment to her husband.

Restless and bored, she sat at their yellow Formica kitchen table and pored over women's magazines for a business idea she could launch from home. Lillian had a brainstorm . . . to advertise custom monogrammed belts and purses in *Seventeen* magazine. Both items were manufactured in her father's leather goods factory. Using their wedding gift money, she took out a one-sixth-page advertisement for $495 and waited for the responses.

## ▶ *A HUNCH LAUNCHES A COMPANY*

Her idea was a huge success, far exceeding Lillian's expectations. Within three months, orders totaled $32,000 and her company, named after the city where they lived, was born, a business that was to be the beginning of Lillian Vernon Corporation.

Testing ads in other magazine came next as Lillian learned what her customers wanted and how best to satisfy them. Trial and error coupled with long hours and a love of work kept Lillian going even after the birth of her first son, Fred. Her part-time "hobby" soon became her passion. The financial rewards were satisfying and she loved planning, selecting items to advertise and fulfilling orders for her customers. In 1954, her business had outgrown its home base so Lillian moved into her first real office, a fourteen square foot space behind her husband's family store. She also rented a nearby storefront as a shipping location and hired her first part-time help. Soon after, she invited her husband, Sam, to join the thriving business full-time as president earning $100 per week. Lillian took the title of vice president at $50 per week, a disparity in salary levels typical of the 1950's.

In October 1956, after several miscarriages, the family grew along with their business. Lillian gave birth to her second son, David, a moment of great joy and celebration. Time with her children was an important part of the family routine even in the midst of the growth of the business, which began to serve new and more sophisticated consumer markets.

By 1958, seven years after that first *Seventeen* ad, the company had sales of $500,000 and offered an expanded product line including monogrammed bookmarks, towels, sweater guards, gloves and jewelry. The addition of a custom jewelry line opened doors to major new business opportunities and the creation of a wholesale division to serve companies including Spencer Gifts and Revlon cosmetics. Through it all, Lillian and Sam lived carefully and invested their profits back into their business to nurture its growth.

Lillian enjoyed traveling across America and abroad looking for unusual items that her customers needed or wanted at affordable prices. She always carried a notebook with her to write down ideas and product information, a habit she continues today.

Mail order shopping was dominated by the big books like Sears Roebuck and Montgomery Ward catalogs. Women were entering the workforce in growing numbers so the efficiency of mail order shopping and the many timesaving products sold by Lillian fueled the growth of their business.

The company grew along with the family. Trips to the zoo, parties, skiing, tennis, sailing and board games were highlights of family life as both the parents and children enjoyed their time together.

By the early 1960's, the company had diversified, manufacturing its own line of products, and moving to a much larger building. Lillian Vernon began publishing its first catalog, which was black and white and just 32 pages, featuring 175 items priced between one and three dollars. After a mailing to 125,000 customers, the first catalog, which cost five cents each to produce, generated a huge response. Orders poured in and extra part-time help, mostly mothers and homemakers, was hired to fill orders. This growth spurt created the need for more space. Soon a 5,000 square foot warehouse became home to her thriving business.

There were many challenges along the way. As a woman, Lillian had the advantage of understanding and knowing her customers' wants and needs. But she also endured the discrimination of financial institutions against women-owned businesses and the loneliness of being one of the few women entrepreneurs at the time. The death of her father and life- time mentor, business pressures, a costly accident in the warehouse and daily challenges were painful chapters in her life. In 1969, Lillian and

Sam were divorced. Sam retained their wholesale business, worth about $5 million in sales and Lillian kept the ownership of the catalog division whose sales were under $1 million annually, but whose success was her passion.

It was a bittersweet time for Lillian who was sad and anxious over the end of her marriage but energized by her new start in life. She threw herself into her work and the role of a single parent. Her struggle to keep family and work balanced became a learning experience as Lillian's business and staffing needs grew. She realized flexible hours and a supportive work environment would attract a huge untapped labor pool of homemakers and mothers who required flexible schedules. Tuition reimbursement, four-month maternity leaves, birthday celebrations, employee recognition awards and company picnics and parties created a nurturing environment, which kept her employees happy.

## ▶ ONE MILLION DOLLARS IN SALES

By 1970, sales hit $1million and entered a period of tremendous growth. Sales doubled in 1973 and 1974 and jumped to $6 million in 1976. By 1982, the momentum had driven the company annual revenues to $60 million.

With growth came new challenges. In 1983, new organizational strategies were needed to keep track of the workforce of 650 people in five different buildings. Rapid growth strained the company's computer systems and finances. In 1987, a competitor filed an antitrust lawsuit against the company for "monopoly" on the sale of custom Christmas ornaments. Lillian Vernon won the lawsuit. Careful attention to detail, a commitment to meet customers' needs, value pricing and friendly, speedy service are among the company's reasons for success.

Company sales reached $100 million in 1986. Lillian decided that the time was right to take the company public on the American Stock Exchange. The initial public offering (IPO) in August 1987 offered 1,900,000 shares selling at $15 each. Lillian Vernon Corporation became the first female-founded company to go public on the American Stock Exchange. Lillian's two sons joined her in the business.

Fifty-one years after her $2000 investment to launch her business, Lillian serves as chairman of the $287 million company which markets 6000 gift, house wares, gardening, Christmas and children's products in eight catalog titles and on two web sites www.lillianvernon.com and www.ruedefrance.com. Free personalization continues to be a Lillian Vernon trademark. From its simple kitchen table beginnings, the company has grown to a staff of 1000, which expands to 5300 people during the Christmas season.

The corporate headquarters is a two-story, glass facility in Rye, a suburb of New York City where 175 are employed. The bulk of the company's operation is centered in Virginia Beach at their one million square foot National Distribution Center. A seasonal call center operates in New Rochelle, New York. Fifteen outlet stores now serve customers in locations along the East Coast from South Carolina to New York.

Lillian's biggest challenge was running her business while taking care of her home and family. As her company grew, she was able to hire a housekeeper, which was a great help. She faced much discrimination in a male-dominated workplace. Today, her biggest challenge is to grow her business in a competitive industry with 12,000 other catalog titles and 25,000 web-sites. The marketplace now demands increasingly unique products and marketing to stand out from the competition.

Lillian's greatest career accomplishment was taking her company public. However, her definition of success goes beyond her career. She says, *"Success is having confidence in your capabilities and talents and living your life to the fullest, sharing your good fortune with others and acknowledging their efforts."*

Secrets of success she would like to share with other women business owners:

- *"Have passion for your work and don't let anything stand in the way of your dream."*
- *"Be practical. Have a business plan and follow it."*
- *"Spend wisely and keep good records."*
- *"Be prepared to accept demands on your time and to make hard choices."*
- *"Most of all, know your customer's needs and never let go of your entrepreneurial spirit, now matter how big your company becomes."*

What's ahead for this business leader? Lillian Vernon continues to enjoy traveling the world in search of new merchandise and guiding her business to the next level. Public speaking and serving on non-profit boards keeps her schedule busy. She has no plans to retire, but she has put more balance into her work and personal life. A physical fitness regimen, philanthropy, a love of fine restaurants and culture, and wonderful friends keep her days filled with excitement.

Lillian's life story can be read in greater detail in her autobiography, *An Eye For Winners: How I Built One of America's Greatest Direct Mail Businesses.*

> *"Business is all about building great relationships."*

**Barbara Baekgaard and Patricia Miller**

# *Vera Bradley Designs*

Popular wisdom tells us: "Don't mix business with pleasure" and "Never go into business with a friend." But Barbara Bradley Baekgaard and Patricia Miller, co-founders of Vera Bradley Designs, have beaten the odds and are having a terrific time as friends running a highly successful company.

In 1976, Pat and her five-year old son arrived at Barbara's

Wildwood Park home in Fort Wayne, Indiana as part of the neighborhood welcoming committee to meet and greet the new neighbors. Little did they know, as Pat rang the doorbell, that together they would eventually create Vera Bradley Designs, a thriving enterprise that would achieve annual sales in the eight figure range by the year 2000.

That summer day, Pat was pleased to meet Barbara and learn that she was a brilliant interior decorator. Barbara confided that due to her husband's career, she had acquired much experience redecorating her own home every several years as a result of corporate relocations. In addition, she had established a small interior design consulting practice with decorating assignments that frequently resulted in clients requesting wallpaper-hanging services. At that time, the most profitable work Barb undertook was actually her wallpaper hanging projects.

When the new neighbor friends shared interests and a cup of coffee that first day, Barbara asked Pat: "Can you hang wallpaper?" Soon the two began to plan to work together on their first venture, a wallpapering service called "Up Your Wall." Their joint venture was the perfect match for two "stay-at-home" moms who wanted the balance of part-time work that fit around their children's schedules and family obligations.

Several years passed. The children grew and another business opportunity presented itself. A friend of Barbara's from Cleveland, Ohio, had hosted a home party Trunk Show for Dunn Worthington, then an upscale preppy clothing line for women sold through home shows in Ohio. The show hostess earned commission and (most important to Pat and Barb) could buy the clothing at a 40% discounted price. After written inquiries, they learned that the Ohio company was not interested in out of state shows. Samples had to be transported by car each week to the next show hostess. Undaunted, the partners drove to Ohio for a meeting to discuss the prospects of a "test show" in Indiana. The only slot available was Thanksgiving week, which typically netted such a poor turnout that the trunk samples were available. With a promise to drive to Ohio the weekend before Thanksgiving to pick up the clothing, a test case deal was struck. The samples would have to be driven 250 miles back to Ohio that same week after the show.

Dunn Worthington hit the jackpot as Pat and Barbara broke all of their records for previous home sales. Despite the inconvenience of moving samples such great distance, the partners convinced the clothing company to schedule three more Indiana trunk shows, all of which were very successful.

In 1982, the partner's creativity and business instincts came together again for another great idea. That February, they were traveling to visit Barbara's parents, Ed and Vera Bradley, in Florida for a week-long vacation to celebrate Ed's 75th birthday. As they sat in the Atlanta airport waiting to change planes, the women noticed how unattractive most of the women traveler's luggage and carry-ons were. Dark colors, masculine designs, more rugged types of duffels and totes were all they could see. It occurred to them that women might enjoy more attractive, feminine or colorful totes, duffels and garment bags. The team that took Dunn Worthington by surprise knew that they had great interior design sense and business skills. They decided to take immediate action to test their hunch on this product and create a selection of sample totes to test market the concept.

Within 24 hours of their return trip, they began their work. Both pitched in $250 to purchase 200 yards of attractive print fabrics, created a prototype tote design and commissioned the alteration lady they worked with for the Trunk Shows to sew 20 totes. Although Barbara was an accomplished seamstress, time was of the essence. The plan was to offer these totes for purchase at the next Dunn Worthington home sale. To keep the test case valid, the partners decided not to tell anyone these were their creation. Instead they created a neutral name and professional label to test the market.

Vera Bradley was the chosen name for the new product line, since the idea was born during their travel to see Vera Bradley, Barbara's mother. Today, the company name warms the heart of both founders as Vera, truly a great lady by their accounts, passed away in 1992. Her persistence, sense of humor, good nature and sense of style live on in the memory of those who knew her well. In fact, Vera had actually been trained in high fashion in the Elizabeth Arden organization. Both founders kiddingly refer to their own impeccable sense of style and appreciation of beauty as "the Vera gene."

The stage was set and the Vera Bradley handbags were offered at the Dunn Worthington Trunk Show in March of 1982. An instant hit, all 20 bags sold immediately and a new company, Vera Bradley Designs, was born. "Where do we go from here?' was the question of the hour. To meet production demand, Pat wrote letters to fabric houses in New York City requesting information on bulk fabric purchases and available lines. But all of her letters were met with silence . . . no replies. The partners knew they could not buy fabric at retail prices and turn a profit, so Barbara tried another approach. During a visit with her daughter, who was a college student at Marymount College in Tarrytown, New York, Barbara decided to take a side trip and visit fabric houses in New York City. An impromptu meeting with Leo Driscoll, who was President of V.I.P. Fabrics, was a lucky break for the new business. Leo guided them on fabric buying and helped them manage their limited startup finances. He remains a good friend today.

About this time the partners decided to apply for a $2000 loan for the business. Barbara and Pat did not feel a strong connection with the first loan officer assigned to them. Even though they were a new and very small business, they decided to ask the bank for a new officer. Both women knew that they could not succeed with the negative attitude of the person they had met. The bank agreed to assign a new loan officer and that individual became a great supporter and business mentor.

Another advisor who deserves mention is George Cook, a gentleman who was a recently retired Vice President of Finance from Rea Magnet Wire in Fort Wayne. George was a volunteer with SCORE—the Service Corps of Retired Executives, a branch of the Small Business Administration that helps startup companies. He was very helpful early on in guiding Pat and Barbara on the steps needed to create and finance a business. While Pat had taught business courses to high school students for six years as a young woman, she found his real world, practical guidance to be an important foundation for their future success. Pat reflects: "I carried all of my business files in a box to meet with George. He was a terrific help to us as new entrepreneurs."

Rather than following a home party strategy, the founders went straight to large-scale retail stores, contacting boutiques directly and selling wholesale at the Chicago Gift Show. They sold to stores throughout the United States. Sales in the first year were $10,000. The second year topped $300,000. By 1985, the company hit $1 million in sales.

In the early years, Vera Bradley was launched from Barbara's home. The business actually started in the basement and later took over much of the first floor. Stock and supplies eventually overran Barbara's family. In 1984, it was time for a move into a rented office. During this time there were still only two employees—the founders of the business. Long hours, hands-on work, and sleepless nights marked the early years as both founders pitched in and created the business day by day. Barbara reflects that they would have had longer office hours, but the space had to be locked at the same time as the primary business. With the pressure of a new business, both owners considered this a blessing in disguise since they had to take a break and leave the building. While work often came home to be completed after dinner, the much-needed family time kept the founders from going into burnout.

On another note, Vera Bradley Designs has been the seed for many other women-owned businesses. From the start and still today, all of the necessary sewing has been contracted to independent sewing companies. One Ohio-based company is owned and operated by a woman and has grown into a large production facility.

Demand continued in the market. Likewise, the company continued to grow. By 1987, it was clear that Vera Bradley needed another new home. The partners decided to build a low-rise flex-space office building in a Fort Wayne industrial park. At first they used part of the building space and leased another section. But as their staff grew to nearly 100 employees, additions have been built to increase the facility to over 24,000 square feet. Here, business, sales and marketing functions take place, along with product research and development, fabric warehousing and component cutting. All shipping of finished goods to

Vera Bradley's national and international retailers also occurs from this location.

Today, Vera Bradley Designs offers a complete line of quilted cotton luggage, handbags, accessories, and table linens in exclusive cotton fabric designs with distinctive border trims. Function, quality and fashion are synonymous with the Vera Bradley products—collected by many women who look forward to the new designs released twice a year along with their seasonal limited edition lines. Provincial Red, Maison Blue, Elizabeth and Blue Toile are but a few in the family of designs with the classic "Vera look." A two-year guarantee ensures buyers that any new print will be available for two years so that ensemble pieces and accessories can be purchased over time in specialty gift shops and boutiques throughout the United States and abroad.

Along with new seasonal quilted cotton prints, Vera Bradley has recently offered limited editions of special silk and microfiber handbags for a day-to-evening look. Additional specialty items have been introduced occasionally, including nylon-covered rolling luggage, teddy bears and Vera Bradley's "Our Favorite Recipes" cookbook—all sold through individual retail stores.

## ▶ FAMILY RIPPLES

Big success stories in business often have a big impact on family life. Vera Bradley Designs definitely changed the lives of its founders and their families. But the ripple effect of this new phenomenon was typically gentle as the business grew up gradually from its infancy into development as a mature business. When the founders' children were younger, the new company had little overhead and could be flexible to meet the family needs. Since it was one year before there were any employees other than founders on payroll, there was no pressure to cover such costs by working at a frenzied pace.

The college age children in both owners' families were actively involved in the business, promoting and selling Vera Bradley handbags and totes on campus. While both moms were highly focused on their work, they tried to keep balance in their lives and hold that mix of achievement and personal life as a model for their children.

## ▶ SUCCESS SECRETS

As the company has grown and prospered, the business community has taken notice. Among their outstanding list of credentials, Vera Bradley Designs has earned the Entrepreneur of the Year Award in their region in both 1987 and 1999, and the Indiana University President's Circle Award in 2000.

The founders of this high profile business have been asked to tell the secrets behind their success. Both women are quick to reply: *"It's all about people."* Early mentors, family and friends, vendors, distributors and the Vera Bradley employees are the foundation that Barbara and Pat agree have made their journey possible and satisfying. Both women are committed to building great interpersonal and business relationships. Their upbeat and caring attitudes are obvious to everyone they encounter.

Pat reflects: *"Our success has been founded on our choice of great people to work with. We have a terrific team."* Co-founder Barbara shares her sentiments: *"Business is really all about building great relationships. Women are typically very good at that. People are important to us."*

The smiles on headquarters' largely female staff, who are all treated as key players on the team, are evidence that the founders' words are put into action every day. Staffers . . . or their wives, also get to try out new handbag designs on a regular basis at no charge. A company perk, many find this adds to their fun and involvement.

While neither woman started their careers hoping to be entrepreneurs, they do have success secrets to share with others who might pursue this path.

### From Pat Miller:

*"Beverly Sills sums up: you can have it all, just not all at once."*
*"Half of life is showing up. Stay open and try new things."*
*"Take calculated risks, follow your instincts, but push yourself."*
*"Being a woman in business can be an asset if you find a way to make it work."*
*"Just do it. Follow your dream."*

### From Barbara Baekgaard:

*"Sell yourself first, your company second, and your product third . . . great advice I learned from my Dad."*
*"Better to try and fail than never to try at all."*
*"Allow other people to help you along the way."*
*"Keep a sense of humor and follow your passion in life."*
*"Become friends with your customers and make a difference in people's lives."*

Vera Bradley's founders have made a big difference in people's lives as creators of the Vera Bradley Golf and Tennis Classic, an annual fundraiser for breast cancer research. The event was created in memory of Mary Sloan, a lifetime friend who worked with Pat and Barbara as a Vera Bradley representative and died of breast cancer in 1992. Her death inspired this impressive tournament to benefit women with breast cancer, an event that has raised nearly $2 million for breast cancer research and programs. To further their commitment, Barbara and Pat created the Vera Bradley Foundation for Breast Cancer in 1998. They made a five-year $1.2 million pledge to endow a chair in oncology at the Indiana School of Medicine in Indianapolis. The pledge will be met ahead of schedule in 2002.

What's on the horizon for these two high-energy women? Both reply that every year is their most exciting year. Although both have grandchildren and enjoy sports and other interests, "retirement" is not in their vocabulary. After years as homemakers and now as highly successful businesswomen, they have learned to balance their lives. They enjoy their personal growth along with the growth of their company. Busy, happy, energized—both founders agree that life is good. While both women make their success story look easy, they confide that it took time, personal discipline, patience, commitment, hard work, a team spirit and a great product to bring them to this place in their lives.

Today Pat and Barbara agree that their biggest challenge is to plan for continued growth of the substantial organization that Vera Bradley Designs has become. New products, new strategies, new markets, a new headquarters are all possibilities they evaluate for the future. Longtime partners and friends, the founders of Vera Bradley Designs will continue to find new achievements as they pull together to sustain and grow their life work for the company they love.

*"Do the right thing and the rest will follow."*

**Gun Denhart**

# Hanna Andersson

Gun Denhart was born and raised in Lund, Sweden, a university town 10 miles northeast of Malmo. Gun's late father, Gunnar Brime, ran a packaging firm. Her mother, Elsa, was a Red Cross volunteer. Gun was the third of four children in her family. She was a pretty girl with an independent and athletic way about her. In spite of her good looks and above average intelligence, Gun was painfully shy.

Life was good in Sweden as Gun was growing up. Like the rest of the world at that time, children were expected to study hard, do well in school and amuse themselves with their friends and school sports in their free time. That was Gun's experience and that of her brother and sisters. At the end of high school, she went on in her studies at Lund University and in 1967 she earned a degree that would be the equivalent of a master's in business administration degree (MBA) in the United States.

After graduation, Gun began teaching business law. In 1969, she wed the owner of an international language school. Within several years, the couple had a child, Philip. Unfortunately, in 1973 the marriage ended and Gun moved to Paris with her two and a half-year-old son.

After a time, she met and fell in love with Tom Denhart, an American working in France who was a television commercial producer for a French advertising agency. In 1975, the couple were married and moved to Greenwich Connecticut where Tom took a position with the Ogilvy & Mather Worldwide advertising firm. Tom's most well known creative work was on the American Express "Don't Leave Home Without It" campaign. At that time, Gun ran the finance department of the United States branch of her ex-husband's international school.

When their son, Christian, was born in 1983, the couple decided it was time to make a change in their lives. They had grown tired of the East Coast pace and wanted to start a business of their own in a part of the country that would allow them a simpler life to raise their family. Gun really hoped to start a venture that had something to do with Sweden. Early on, they considered selling Swedish bottled water or Swedish prefab housing.

The comments of friends and strangers admiring their new baby's colorful outfits, gifts sent from Sweden by Gun's parents, inspired the couple to consider a Swedish baby clothes catalogue. People wanted to know where they could buy such well-made, attractive baby clothes in the United States. At the time, they were just not available except directly from Swedish companies. Gun and Tom decided to fill the market need for all-cotton, high-quality clothes for infants and children. They named their catalogue "Hanna Andersson" after Gun's grandmother, Hanna, who loved children and had sewn many outfits for Gun and her siblings when they were growing up in Sweden.

In 1983, the couple sold their Connecticut home and saved half of the proceeds toward starting a children's clothing catalogue. Tom could count on his salary from his former position for one year, which helped with the decision to try their hand at the new business. They moved to Portland, Oregon, Tom's hometown, bought a large New England-style house, and set to work to start on the Hanna Andersson launch.

Gun's personal experience and knowledge of Swedish clothing, combined with her business background and work experience gave her a head start over many entrepreneurs in understanding what it took to begin a business. Tom's strong background in international advertising and his personal creativity and marketing flair were a perfect combination with Gun's unique skills.

Still, the work ahead was daunting. Gun remembers moving to a new state and a new home with two young children and her husband while they were in the midst of launching the new business. It was overwhelming. She remembers it was a dark, cold November. She didn't know anyone. It was rough getting a new home and life started while starting up the catalogue.

Both Gun and Tom knew the basics of what had to be done and set to work. Tasks were undertaken based on their individual strengths. Gun took care of the business basics including finance, buying, organizing, and setting up the systems that would be needed. Tom handled the catalogue creation and marketing. Fortunately, as they were learning about their business, there was not another company doing exactly what they were doing.

When it was time to prepare the first catalogue, the couple went back to Sweden with their children and set about taking needed photographs, planning copy, and working with a Swedish printer to have the production completed. One of Gun's friends was a woman who worked out of her home as a business writer. The children of both women would play as the mothers worked over catalogue layouts. This process continued for the first four or five years because it was less costly than the resources they found closer to home. Later, the catalogue work was moved to the United States. Interestingly, Gun's eldest son would later prepare a catalogue for a toy company when he was just a teenager. No stranger to business, he was exposed early on to the family trade.

In 1984, the first catalogue was printed. To enhance their first mailing, Tom and Gun cut out and glued one-square-inch fabric samples into 75,000 catalogues. This process was used for the first three introductory catalogues. Gun and Tom bought customer lists and took out small ads in parents' magazines asking interested customers to call for a catalogue of the Swedish clothes. The very first ad slogan was "Why are Swedish Babies So Happy?" Customers remember this advertisement to this day.

Sales started right away. Within six months, they had sold $53,000 in clothing. People really liked the soft fabrics and bright colors. Clothes were selected for the collection with children in mind, from big buttons and pull-on styles to make it easy for toddlers to dress themselves to kid-proof, reinforced knees and soft fabrics that feel good against the skin. Young mothers started talking about the products. Word of mouth played a big part in the new line's introduction. In the second year, the business started to make a profit much to the Denhart's relief. By the end of that year, sales topped the one million-dollar mark. The company was officially launched.

Their Portland home was headquarters for the new business. It was a roomy old structure. Gun's office was in an upstairs extra room. Tom's was in a former porch that had been enclosed. Kitchen table meetings were the routine. Two garages housed inventory and shipping equipment. An attached garage was the most convenient of these. The other was an older structure that was uphill, presenting a challenge when carrying or dragging large boxes of clothing inventory there for storage.

Tom and Gun agreed that it was more appropriate for Gun to serve as spokesperson and chief executive for the company. Her role as a woman was most fitting as the company voice. (After seven years, Tom who was always a creative genius grew tired of the business and took early retirement due to health concerns.)

Within two years, the Hanna Andersson catalogue business had 20 employees and outgrew the Denhart's home. As exciting as this was to move into a 9000 square foot downtown commercial space, it was an exhausting time. It was the week between

Christmas and New Year's. Every stick of clothing and furniture had to be moved. They decided not to hire movers but to move everything themselves with their staff. It was a low point, Gun recalls as she and their staff worked until they dropped. She remembers standing with a coworker while both of them cried. They finally decided to stop and go home.

One would think the new space would hold them for a while. Within one year, though, they outgrew it. Tom saw this coming and went looking for a new location. He found an old 1921 vintage, five-story brick warehouse building that was owned by the bank in a rough part of town. The 55,000 square foot building was for sale. Gun asked him if he was just kidding or just crazy? It seemed like a big bite for the new company, but it was a deal they just couldn't pass up. Moving day came again. This time, they moved into two floors of their own building. As the company grew and needed expansion room they eventually added floors until the entire building was used by the catalogue business.

This location is still home for Hanna Andersson today. Over the years, the neighborhood it is situated in has been refurbished. It is now a popular office area for advertising agencies, businesses and shops. Once again, Gun and Tom were ahead of their time.

## ▶ NEW HORIZONS TO THE EAST

Gun's son, Philip, chose to study in Tokyo, Japan for a year after he graduated from high school and before attending college. It was 1989. Philip thought Japan would be a great new market for Hanna Andersson clothes. On a trip to visit Philip there, Gun and he undertook some small research work to explore whether or not there was opportunity. She took out a small ad there to generate new sales potential in this market. This first step started their Japanese market, which grew into one million dollars in sales during its first year offering the mail order line.

Three years later, Gun returned to Japan, this time with the Committee of 200, an exclusive group of women business owners and senior executives throughout the world. The trip was an educational experience about Japanese business for the women's group. Gun found that she traveled to Japan often. On one occasion she was asked to give a presentation at a United Nations sponsored conference held for 400 Japanese women interested in becoming entrepreneurs. At the end of the scheduled conference time, Gun invited a number of her Japanese customers to join her to discuss further her products and enjoy a dialogue about what products and services people desired. This type of exchange of ideas has kept Gun in touch with her customers in every market. Today, sales in Japan comprise about 20 percent of her business, which is annually in the $60 million range.

## ▶ NO FEAR

For many people, it is hard to imagine the many new paths Gun Denhart has walked throughout her life. She left her native country and moved to France. Later, she moved to the United States and lived in several states there. She started a new business with her husband when her two children were very young. Many of us cannot imagine doing one of these things much less all of them.

When asked about what prepared her for such independent pursuits as an adult, Gun looks back on some of her childhood experiences. As a young child, about ten years in age, Gun remembers being very competitive in a Swedish community program that sold brightly colored paper flowers in May to raise money for local charities. To give her sales a boost, she borrowed an antique pram from a local museum and sold a record share in her town. Great recognition from the community was the only reward for her young, creative effort.

On another occasion, she recalls an instance when she and a friend decided to bring Gun's new pony into town from its stable in the country at a local farmer's place. It was a nice summer day and the two eleven year olds decided they would just walk the 45-mile distance to the city. Gun shares that it is about a 50 minute drive today. Without incident, the girls showed up in the center of town, pony and all. Once there, they decided to give rides to their friends in the neighborhood for a small riding fee. Subsequently, Gun's parents decided to stable the horse in town after her long walk.

Independent, creative, entrepreneurial, Gun has taken risks along the way, but they have certainly paid off. Her advice to other women would-be entrepreneurs is to put fears aside and try to reach your goals if they are important to you. *"Don't be afraid to fail and end up never trying. Even failure and mistakes teach us valuable lessons. It may be difficult as a woman to get where you want to be, but try before you let your hopes pass by,"* she urges.

## ▶ A GENEROUS SPIRIT

Hanna Andersson has been in the news frequently regarding its philanthropic policies. While the exact details of the programs have changed from time to time, Gun has given back an enormous amount of time, energy, and dollars to community causes over the years. Her spirit is clearly as generous as it is independent. The company donates 5% of its pretax dollars to charity and encourages volunteerism among its employees, paying for their volunteer time off. Childcare is also subsidized for company employees. Gun believes, "You can't focus on your work if you don't feel secure about where your child is."

Causes supported by Hanna Andersson include the American Heart Association as recipient of proceeds from sales of the "Have A Heart Long Johns"; Oregon's SMART Program which teaches children from kindergarten to third grade through reading tutors; "Cash For Kids" which makes a charitable donation to schools of employees' children; and "Stand For Children" an advocacy group for children's health and well-being.

The most well known of the company's philanthropic commitments is its own award-winning "Hannadowns" program that recycles used Hanna Andersson children's clothing to less fortunate little ones. Two charitable partners now receiving and distributing Hannadowns are the Massachusetts Coalition for the Homeless and the Hamilton Family Center. Customers are encouraged to hand down their used "hannas" to the needy in their own communities as well.

## ▶ GOING FORWARD

Eighteen years after the first catalogue was launched, Hanna Andersson is alive and well offering Swedish-quality clothing for children in soft, durable 100% cotton. Five issues of the catalogue are mailed per year featuring spring, summer, fall, winter and holiday apparel for babies, girls, boys and women, along with a number of gift selections. There is now a distribution center in Louisville, Kentucky. Retail stores are located in Portland Oregon and White Plains, New York and outlet stores are open for business in Maine, Minnesota, Indiana and Oregon. There is also a Japanese call center in Tokyo, Japan.

The company mission remains essentially the same as it was in the first years of business: "To market clothes to enhance the lives of our customers through quality, functionality, durability and design. We celebrate our beliefs with integrity. Our culture bears witness to our values. Our participation confirms our responsibility to the larger community."

The company web site, www.hannaAndersson.com, is the sales channel for 25% of the overall business. One of the early users of Internet distribution, the company has found many customers prefer to order on-line rather than through telephone orders.

When asked what the biggest challenge is in the future for the thriving company, Gun replied, *"Our greatest challenge is to be a small, privately held company in a world where businesses are constantly consolidating into bigger and bigger organizations."* Her advice to other entrepreneurs, *"Do the right thing and the rest will follow."*

Gun will no doubt manage to make her company size an asset even in the face of growing competition. She has outgrown her shyness and become a savvy, independent entrepreneur. Internationally respected and acknowledged by *Working Woman* magazine as among the Top 500 women-owned businesses today and by *Working Mother* as one of the 85 best companies for women employees, Gun Denhart's Hanna Andersson evolution will continue to be a story to watch.

> "The more
> you believe
> that people
> can do,
> the more
> they do."
>
> ——————
>
> **Margaret
> Johnsson**

# The Johnsson Group, Inc.

When Margaret Johnsson was a five year old towhead playing in the neighborhood with her friends, she told anyone who asked her what she wanted to be when she grew up, that she would own a company one day. She did not know what kind of company at the time, but she was sure she would own one. It appears a little girl's dreams can become a grown woman's reality.

The daughter of a schoolteacher and a social worker, Margaret came from well-educated, highly principled stock. Her parents believed deeply in the importance of their work and they realized their choices were based on commitment to humanity not personal financial gain. But entrepreneurism ran strong in the Johnsson family line as well. Her great uncle, grandfather and both grandmothers were all business owners in their time. Margaret knew from childhood that she would one day own a business of her own. As a young adult she promised herself that she would reach this dream by the time she was 30 years old.

Margaret's career path really opened up when she was just 16. The owner of a local construction company in the Chicago area approached her high school principal to find an honors student that would work after school for his firm to help him and learn the business. Margaret was approached by the principal and reluctantly went for the interview. At the time she was working as a waitress and making good money for a young girl.

Jerry Kipley was the president of a family-owned business, Kipley Construction. He worked long hours and was looking for a low-cost way to finish up his work earlier in the day and spend more time with his family in the evenings. His search for a young assistant who was a quick study appeared to be over when Margaret arrived. But she was not convinced immediately that this opportunity was one she wanted. Jerry offered her minimum wage with a promise of increasing her paycheck as her responsibilities grew. Still, Margaret was making quite a bit more than minimum wage as a part-time waitress. Reluctantly, she agreed to give the after school job a try. If it didn't work out, she planned to quit and be a lifeguard the next summer.

Jerry immediately began teaching Margaret about the business. Her assignments included typing, attending meetings with Jerry and taking notes, filing and other assorted jobs. Basically, she did whatever basic tasks needed to be done. At the end of two weeks, she took on the job of handling the payroll. It seemed Mrs. Kipley had been having difficulty reconciling the numbers. Margaret found the work to be easy for her. This was her first exposure to accounting. It was also her first raise in pay. Within two weeks her boss increased her pay as he had promised. Margaret took to business like a duck to water. She was a natural.

Margaret Johnsson worked for Jerry Kipley for two years during high school while learning everything she could about the business. She became such an asset to the company that Jerry asked her to stay on during college and agreed to pay her tuition to the University of Illinois in downtown Chicago if she would keep working at the construction company. She took the deal and worked her classes around work requirements.

As time went on, Margaret became a junior project manager and took on responsibilities in project planning, negotiation, and implementation. A favorite story involves her work securing construction permits at Chicago City Hall. One of the very few women who appeared in the permit office at that time, Margaret often pulled a "Superman" routine, changing from blue jeans or school clothes to a business suit for an appearance asking plan approval from the inspectors or the zoning board. After a while, the folks at City Hall knew she was on a tight schedule and would invite her to come to the head of the line of requesters so that she could return to classes on time. A knowledgeable, attractive young woman was one of a kind in this typically male setting. Margaret Johnsson was already building a reputation as a hard-working business pioneer.

When she graduated from college, she was asked to stay on at Kipley Construction, but Margaret declined the offer. After all, she still held on to her dream of owning her own business, a goal that Jerry encouraged her to pursue. While a student in downtown Chicago, she had savored the view of the Chicago skyline and the city lights and vowed that she would work in big business in a corporate setting. Her first career job was a position with Beatrice, an organization that was a multi-billion dollar conglomerate owning a number of other entities from food to rental car companies. She chose Beatrice for the exposure it would give her to many types of companies. If she never saved enough to start her own business, she figured she just might get to run one of theirs. (Jerry had advised her that she would need to save one year's salary before she started up a company of her own.)

Margaret was accustomed to hard work and with six years of business experience with Kipley behind her, she rose quickly through the Beatrice ranks in a program that offered a broad management training experience. She worked in Operations Analysis, which included internal audit accounting functions and operational consulting on a number of strategic teams. Here she found tremendous exposure to business problems and solutions that worked.

When asked if the "glass ceiling" concept in traditional big business was a factor in motivating Margaret, her answer was "no". She had not gone that far into her career yet. At the time, she was just starting out and moving up on a fast track. The sky was still the limit. The pace was hectic but the travel was exciting and the world of big business still alluring. Until her Beatrice career move, she had not experienced her first airplane trip. Now, her world was huge.

In 1985, Kohlberg, Kravis Roberts & Co. (KKR) investment-banking firm took over Beatrice ownership and the corporate company strategy changed. Margaret was highly regarded by company management and therefore received many stretch opportunities under the new ownership. She was one of four people who worked on the divestiture of Avis Rent-A-Car. The confidence, knowledge and experience Margaret brought to the table were recognized even as a young businessperson just 25 years old. But she still didn't think she had found her life work. She wondered if graduate school would shed some light on a new direction.

Still following her dream, Margaret took a job with Kraft for more big business exposure and the opportunity to have her employer pay for graduate studies at Northwestern University where she earned a master's degree in management. Studying at night while working full-time at Kraft, the schedule was rigorous. Working hours were often from 7:00 am to 10:00 pm or later if the assignment required it.

From time to time, her old boss and mentor, Jerry, would call her and ask her if she was running Kraft yet. If she wasn't running Kraft, he wondered why she was still there? She also wondered how she would reach her dream.

## ▶ *TIME TO TAKE THE PLUNGE*

At age 29 and a half, Margaret decided to take the plunge and dive into her own business ownership. She did not have a full year's wages saved but she had enough credit to live a full year on credit cards. She knew if she didn't quit, she wouldn't have the time or energy to find a company to run. She thought she'd just figure out the next step after she quit.

In June of 1991, she began consulting for many of her former Beatrice and Kraft contacts to earn money, while exploring an international list business that she was interested in pursuing. By the end of 12 months, she realized her consulting business was keeping her afloat financially while the list business research was proving it to be a lost cause. It occurred to her then that perhaps she should start a consulting business since she found ample work and had great success with it. Gradually, she found more work than she could handle and brought on other consultants to join her in fulfilling assignments.

By 1993, the work was coming in strong enough that Margaret decided to change the status of her six independent freelance consultants into permanent employees. She could see a heavy calendar of work ahead for the next six months. It was time to take the next step with full-time staff and office space. Ironically, many of these same employees had worked with Margaret at Beatrice and Kraft. Some of them were her superiors or direct boss.

Billings grew as the company did. Annual billings in 1992 were $60,000. In 1993, the Johnsson Group billed about $250,000. The following year the consulting group brought in $500,000. By 1995 the firm hit one million dollars in annual billing. Today, the company bills about $11 million annually and has 50+ full-time employees.

# ▶ *HOME SWEET CROWDED HOME*

Throughout this journey into business ownership, Margaret proceeded cautiously with her overhead. She started the business out of her one bedroom apartment in downtown Chicago. Specifically, the Johnsson Group began in Margaret's living room, later expanding into her dining room, bedroom and every room in the house except the bathroom. Piles of papers surrounded her bed. She had to leap over them every night when it was time to get some sleep. She could no longer see the fireplace in her apartment as it was obscured by the file cabinets in front of it, along with several desks placed in the living room for extra staff. So abused was this living space, when Margaret finally rented offices for her company, she moved from the apartment also to get away from its memories of clutter and work.

Margaret's mom was her secretary in the early days and worked in the apartment answering phones for free. She would come to the apartment and answer phones, using her maiden name to appear more business like. Her mom's name was Margaret too. The senior Ms. Johnsson has a young sounding telephone voice. Ironically, callers would often ask Margaret who the young girl was that she had working for her at the time. The mother daughter team has great memories of their work together.

When the Johnsson Group moved from their crowded quarters to commercial space, they moved to loft offices on the west side of the Loop in downtown Chicago, then a low-rent district in the city. As their business grew, the firm took over more space until they finally outgrew the available offices. Finally, they moved again to an office building in the heart of the Chicago Loop financial district, where they are located now. With Margaret's many longtime friends in the construction industry, the offices are quite attractively finished.

## ▶ THE HEART OF THE BUSINESS

A thriving financial consulting business, The Johnsson Group today receives 90% of its work from blue chip Fortune 500 companies. Their specialties include financial analysis, financial process and procedure and internal controls work. Developments that have been catalysts to their growth have included corporate downsizing, much needed Y2K, ERP and other financial systems implementation, acquisition integration assignments, and e-commerce applications for their clients. As business trends and conditions change, their work adapts to the needs of their business clients looking for financial solutions.

Corporate trends fuel any financial business, but The Johnsson Group's competition is among the keenest in the business world including companies that are 100 times their size. The five major national accounting firms including Arthur Andersen, Ernst & Young, PricewaterhouseCoopers, KPMG, and Deloitte and Touche are competing for work with this upstart, savvy firm. What sets The Johnsson Group apart is the depth of experience of their staff, their creativity and their effective skills in implementation of financial strategy. Margaret knew that while many of the large firms wanted to set the strategy for financial plans, few would actually implement with experienced professionals of the caliber of The Johnsson Group. Her experience hiring financial consultants at Beatrice and Kraft showed her there was also a need for fresh approaches and breakthrough thinking to solve financial problems.

Creative solutions are what set The Johnsson Group apart. Margaret studied the creative process and learned that new ideas are usually born in the subconscious mind after the conscious mind has absorbed the basic facts. She was reminded of how many times individuals would claim a new idea came to him or her while driving, showering or relaxing after work.

With this understanding of the creative process, Margaret built her company around a model of "work/life balance" so that her consultants would have time to step back and generate breakthrough thinking in the spaces away from their daily work. The many young, tired consultants and internal professional staff that Margaret had met in her corporate work were often too tired to think, much yet think creatively. This creative professionalism is the hallmark of The Johnsson Group consulting service that Fortune 500 companies have come to appreciate.

Since landing its first national account work with the Quaker Oats Company, the firm's client list has come to include Kraft Foods, Sears Roebuck & Co., CNA Insurance and Baxter Healthcare Corporation, among others. Margaret Johnsson and her firm are also now highly acclaimed in the national and regional business press, including recognition as the Small Business Administration (SBA) Small Business Person of the Year (2001) for the State of Illinois.

## ▶ BALANCING VERSUS JUGGLING

The Johnsson Group walks the talk that they share with their clients. Their consultant employees are encouraged to work flexible schedules to accommodate their family and personal lives, as long as they are bringing high quality consulting back to their work. The commitment of the associates is supported by office policies that allow staff to work four long days and stay home one day a week. The balance of work and life is always the key.

Vacations are earned at one week per year of employment up to five weeks total, while starting with two weeks in the first year. After each three-year period of employment with The Johnsson Group, all employees are required to take a two-week paid sabbatical to a place other than home, to learn and experience new ideas and places as part of a personal growth experience. Margaret approves proposed plans and offers $1000 spending money in addition to the paid time off. Sabbatical weeks are taken in addition to paid vacation days. It is no wonder that The Johnsson Group has no trouble finding qualified professionals and keeping them.

## ▶ ROUGH SLEDDING

Life was not always easy for Margaret while managing the company's growth. External sales required persistence and determination. Internal problems were another matter. At one point, the firm opened a Denver office. Soon this proved to be difficult to run long-distance and was a challenge to staffing in keeping with their work/life balance. The office was eventually closed, despite its immediate financial success.

During one period of tremendous growth in 1994, Margaret brought in a minority (10%) partner to help manage the company. In less than one year, there were terrific problems with this decision and Margaret had to buy out her new partner, a move that proved to be extremely financially costly. The following year, The Johnsson Group actually undertook a turnaround for their own company that was enabled by loans from family and friends to help the firm meet their large payroll requirements.

Twelve months later the young firm was back on solid footing, but in need of bank financing to support its continued growth. A *Wall Street Journal* article featuring the growing firm hit the presses just in time. Up until then, Margaret had financed the business on her personal lines of credit, credit cards and loans from family and friends. Finally, her business was recognized by the banking institutions and a loan was secured that would allow for further growth.

Day to day challenges that The Johnsson Group faced were those every business deals with at some time. Establishing credibility, getting prospects to return a call, selling new business accounts, focusing on new and better ways to offer consulting services, these were among the hurdles that Margaret dealt with early on and continues to work with today. She sees it all as an ongoing process. Each stage has its own lessons to learn.

Bringing in a management team and trusting them to learn and manage is a leap of faith Margaret dealt with as the business moved into higher levels. Making payroll with each burst of new growth was a hurdle her expanding company had to keep in focus. These were lessons Margaret learned early with Jerry Kipley, but they took on new meaning when ultimate responsibility was hers.

## ▶ HAPPY ENDINGS AND BEGINNINGS

All things considered, as demanding as business ownership can be, Margaret enjoys her work and finds it less grueling than the schedule she kept while working at Beatrice and Kraft. Although she is ultimately in charge of her business, her goal is to run her life, not let her life run her. Financial success, in her vision, is the by-product of doing what you want to do and doing it well. Again, her commitment to work/life balance underscores a great business and a great life, by her own account. In her spare time, Margaret enjoys her daughters aged one year and eight and time with her husband, Mike.

When asked for counsel to offer other would be women entrepreneurs Margaret's reply is, *"Never underestimate people. The more you believe people can do, the more they do. The less you believe they can do, the less they do."* On another note she adds, *"Write down your dreams. Believe in yourself and ask for help from others and from God to find strength and persistence."* Margaret keeps a "dream board" with her written goals in her computer files. She is committed to continual improvement for her business and her self. Business mentors and professional peers help guide her future directions.

Of course, Jerry Kipley, her parents, sister, friends and staff have been a support system that was key to The Johnsson Group story. While her father and Jerry Kipley are now deceased, the support and encouragement given to a 16 year old young woman lives on in her success that she defines as *"living life and working on your own terms."*

The dream of a five-year old girl has come a long way in Chicago, Illinois.

# Success Secrets

## CLUSTER TWO—
## *Building Blocks*

▶ *SUCCESS SECRET #5:*
*Women Sell to Other Women Well*

It became apparent in interviewing the Millionaire Women for this collection that over half of these entrepreneurs sold their products to other women. The Pampered Chef, Cookies By Design, Mary Kay Cosmetics, Discovery Toys, Vera Bradley, Hanna Andersson, Lillian Vernon are all companies already profiled in this book that rely heavily and in some cases, almost exclusively, on marketing to women. In subsequent chapters you will read about Schoolbelles, Nature's Choice and Victoria MacKenzie-Childs that also rely heavily on a female buying demographic. This was a phenomenon that has not been the subject of recent marketing texts, but bears serious consideration.

Questions arise as to why this is true. Is it because women understand the wants and needs of other women? Is it because the company's founder has experienced a unique opportunity or need as a woman? Do women, in general, want to support women-owned businesses? Are women more forgiving as consumers, allowing the growing pains of a new business to be worked out while still remaining loyal purchasers?

Anecdotal evidence is all that is available here. There has been scarce marketing research published on this phenomenon. In spite of this lack of scientific study, the fact that women entrepreneurs have served the needs of other women successfully is a success secret worth mentioning for those who might be considering a new business launch.

## ▶ *SUCCESS SECRET #6: Learn, Learn, Learn*

Lifelong learning . . . learning by doing . . . listening, these are primary among the skills that kept repeating themselves in the success stories encountered here. It would appear that there is no substitute for constant learning as new entrepreneurs begin an enterprise and strive to sustain and modify it over the years. Each of the Millionaire Women came to her business with a unique set of skills. Some had business experience. Many did not. Some had management expertise, while others knew their product or service but lacked formal experience managing a team. Whatever knowledge was missing from their experience, these sixteen exceptional women pursued until they could understand and manage their overall business.

Lane Nemeth had virtually no business experience before launching Discovery Toys and had to learn by doing in each stage of the business' growth. She captured her breakthrough thoughts as "Learning Moments" in her own memoirs. Mary Ellen Sheets learned how to run her business through experience that ultimately took Two Men and a Truck into the franchise arena. Mary Carroll had to manufacture an entire school's uniforms twice one year (with the second run gratis), before learning more about commercial grade fabrics and their durability. Mary is an advocate of lifelong learning and surrounds herself with intelligent people from whom she can learn. Every one of these women successes has had to learn about and assess new developments such as the Internet and other innovation to determine the effect on their specific business.

Success rarely comes in a straight-line progression. Trial and error is a large part of the learning process. Arlene Lenarz of Mary Kay Cosmetics describes the experience of breaking through learning barriers when she says: *"we can't enjoy the mountaintops if we have never seen the valleys."* Barbara Baekgaard of Vera Bradley adds, *"It is better to try and fail than never to try at all."* Learning while trying to implement a new dream is at the heart of the growth process.

There is great support for this message of lifelong learning that echoes in the comments of almost all of the Millionaire Women. Noted author Peter Senge who is also the founder and director of the Center for Organizational Learning at MIT's Sloan School of Management is a proponent of the "learning organization" which encourages and empowers all of its members to continually seek new ideas and skills for personal and professional effectiveness. In his book, *The Fifth Discipline: The Art and Practice of the Learning Organization*, Senge details the importance of this process and builds an effective case for it based on a history of results. Steven Covey expands on the principle in his popular bestseller, *7 Habits of Highly Successful People*, in which he proposes that the habit of self-development, "sharpening the saw" in his words, is key to continued success.

The fact that universities, colleges, chambers of commerce, professional associations, and communities offer an expansive curriculum of on-site and online adult learning courses from coast to coast in the United States and abroad seems to substantiate that lifelong learning is a Success Secret worth pursuing and remembering.

## ▶ *SUCCESS SECRET #7: Persistence Pays*

There appears to be no substitute for persistence as these successes were achieved in every case over a period of years. The rise and rapid fall of the dotcom millionaires would appear to validate that overnight success stories seldom last. If it appears to be too good to be true, perhaps it isn't true. In any case, the "overnight" success stories that the Millionaire Women have shared reached major success in most cases over a period of years. Most had some measure of success early on. However, major success in business most often requires a pattern of development and growth. In this environment, persistence at times is everything.

Former United States President, Calvin Coolidge, once said: "Nothing in the world can take the place of persistence. Talent will not; nothing is more common than unsuccessful men with talent. Genius will not; unrewarded genius is almost a proverb. Education will not; the world is full of educated derelicts. Persistence and determination alone are omnipotent. The slogan, 'Press On', has solved and will always solve the problems of the human race."

The Millionaire Women seem to agree with former President Coolidge. In the long haul, it is worth hanging on through the hard times. You will read about Lorraine Tribe in Chapter 16. I think if you ask her about enduring the sale of her home twice to keep her business afloat in hard times, she will share that persistence was well worthwhile in 2001, when she sold her company, Quest Personnel, for four million dollars.

## ▶ *SUCCESS SECRET #8: Business Basics*

### *Planning, Finance, Customers and Staff*

Once an entrepreneur has decided upon a product or service to bring to market, the momentum that drives its ultimate success evolves from good basic business approaches. While sales are possible without this, the full potential of a product is seldom if ever realized without an organized, strategic approach and attention to sound business basics.

**Good basic business advice** is offered by Lillian Vernon. *"Have a written business plan and follow it,"* she urges. When she began Lillian Vernon she started with a product that was unique and that she could afford to produce. She then developed an advertising and distribution approach that was in line with what she could afford and still get the job done. At the kitchen table level, she planned for product, manufacturing, marketing, delivery and accounting, all fundamentals of running an effective business. As her business grew larger, she learned more about human resources and finance considerations. The business functions that were used grew in size and complexity but the basics remained the same.

Here are some other thoughts of this woman who created the first female-founded company to go public on a major stock exchange: *"Spend wisely and keep good records, and don't spend what you don't have."*

**On the subject of customers' needs and wants,** Lillian adds, *"Know your customers' needs; set pricing that reflects the value of the product."* Patricia Miller of Vera Bradley agrees that it is important to *"become friends with your customers to serve them better."* Patricia's partner and co-founder of Vera Bradley, Barbara Baekgaard comments that in dealing with customers *"sell yourself first, your company second and your product, third."* Vera Bradley test markets its products by offering them to employees to use and comment on features and styles that they like as typical customers The company's founders test marketed their handbags prior to officially starting Vera Bradley Design. Market research, while not widely used by the 16 featured Millionaire Women at startup, can be a useful tool for someone exploring the feasibility of a new product. When it comes to what sells and what doesn't, the customer is ultimately always right.

**Finance considerations are critical** to the success of any venture. Startup capital is needed to launch a business, particularly if a product is manufactured. This demand may be less crucial in a professional service industry at startup, although operating capital is always eventually needed. While some of the Millionaire Women turned a profit immediately and never relied on outside financing, others had their own creative approaches to this issue.

Vera Bradley's founders relied on profits from sales after the initial investment of $250 for fabric needed to make their custom totes. Lillian Vernon tapped in to her wedding gift money to buy her first ad in *Seven-*

*teen* magazine and pay for manufacturing of her first product order. Gun Denhart and her husband lived on his severance package from a former employer during the first year of the startup of Hanna Andersson. Lane Nemeth was fortunate to arrange loans from family members on several occasions. Gwen Willhite relied on credit cards, as needed, a tactic that a majority of women-owned businesses still rely on today. Margaret Johnsson, with her finance background, understood the need for capital planning and applied for significant lines of credit prior to the business launch of The Johnsson Group.

Unfortunately, the banking industry has not been historically optimistic or even-handed awarding loans to women entrepreneurs. This appears to be changing, particularly in major metropolitan markets. Some financial institutions now see women entrepreneurs as a market niche and actually court their business as you will note in Barbara Mowat's profile and her "Uniquely Canada" website that has been sponsored by a Canadian bank.

Venture capitalists are another source of funding. None of the Millionaire Women featured here mentioned this as a revenue stream that they used. A February, 2001 presentation by Working Woman Network chief executive officer, Kay Koplovitz, indicates that this financial sector is still woefully behind the times in their appreciation for the clout of women-owned business and, while starting to change, venture capitalists by and large are still slow to fund such companies.

Perhaps the best message to take away in the area of finance is to pay attention to it and to plan for growth in line with the resources that you have access to for your business. Definitely have a solid plan for the dollars needed at launch. Keep your personal and business records separate at all times. And don't grow any faster than you can afford to.

Good business advisors are important, particularly in the area of finance. This has been key to the successes featured in this book. Vera Bradley owners sought financial advice from their banker, their husbands and outside business mentors. Hanna Andersson was launched with the financial and marketing acumen of Gun Denhart's spouse as a bonus to her work with the company. Margaret Johnsson, with her own expertise in the area of finance, still calls on the creativity and perspective of a group of business advisors she has linked into her company's work. All of the Millionaire Women have dealt with finance on their own terms. It is a basic component of every business and with good planning, is a foundation for continued success.

**Appreciation for human resources** is a success secret that was mentioned by all of the Millionaire Women as key to their accomplishment. This business basic has opened doors to increased productivity, hiring opportunities, and efficient staffing, particularly in the organizations that employ women who often appreciate flexible scheduling around family commitments and appreciate the camaraderie and sensitivity a positive human resource approach brings to their work lives.

Part-time help has played an important role in the success of these new businesses that could not handle the pressure of an immediate full-time workforce. The Millionaire Women were tuned into resources that could provide this as evidenced by Lillian Vernon's hiring of working moms, Margaret Johnsson's initial use of freelance help and Rian van Velzen-Bastiaansen's contract labor with a nearby handicapped community center in Holland as noted later in this book.

The level of appreciation and attention to relationships with staff and customers that is exhibited by the Millionaire Women is much higher than that evidenced in many businesses today. "Relationships are everything" is a mantra heard over and over in conversations with this high-performing group of women entrepreneurs. This is evidenced in the way they treat their human resources with careful hiring, frequent recognition, teamwork and celebration of success. Likewise, this relationship theme is evidenced in their dealings with customers, suppliers and their loved ones. (Mary Ellen Sheets' Two Men and a Truck success strategy revolves around the highest levels of empathy and respect for her associates and her customers in the transportation industry, one not usually typified by a warm and caring personality.)

It is obvious that money does not in fact buy everything even at high levels of achievement. Good relationships are a focus and a goal at every level for the Millionaire Women. This human resource or relationship emphasis, however, appears to be a success secret that is integral to the company's mission and corporate culture. It is genuine or it doesn't work. Realizing that sincerity and integrity are companions to this approach is another success secret in its own right.

> *"Do a little every day and you will accomplish a lot."*

**Mary Ellen Sheets**

# Two Men and a Truck

When Mary Ellen Sheets went back to work after her youngest son was two years old, her coworkers called her "Pinkie" because she blushed whenever one of the managers spoke to her. This painfully shy young woman would come a long way over the coming years as she moved from a primary role as "mom" to "chief executive officer" of a multimillion dollar enterprise including a moving company and a top-rated, nationally recognized franchise organization.

Perhaps it was her single parent status that gave her the courage to change and grow. *"It seemed like one day my husband left to buy a loaf of bread and then, he never came back,"* she reflects. With three teenage children, Mary Ellen knew she had to be strong for them and provide a stable home. And that she did. Eventually employed as a systems analyst working for the state of Michigan, she could count on a good income, attractive benefits and five weeks of vacation with pay. In all, life was good and she had survived the exit of her spouse.

Time went on. As her sons, Brigham (Brig) and Jon, grew older, they began using the family's pickup truck to help move things for friends and people in the area. The boys decided to call their part-time business "Two Men and a Truck" and their mom helped out by drawing a makeshift cartoon logo featuring a truck with two stick figures inside. Word spread and Brig and Jon were pleased to earn the extra money as high school teenagers. Eventually, both of the young men enrolled in college attending Northern Michigan University, which was a six to seven hours drive to home near Lansing, Michigan. But unlike most families when the children leave for college, the phone did not stop ringing after they left. Customers continued to call looking for moving help from the trustworthy "two men" and their truck.

In 1985, Mary Ellen decided that with this much demand, she would keep the business going on her own on a part-time basis. She knew by then that she needed a bigger truck though. So she took a chance and spent $350 on an old rundown moving truck that in her own words was truly "a beater". She hired two men to perform the heavy moving work whenever a request came in for moving services. (As of today, this $350 has been the only personal financial contribution she has ever had to make to her successful company.) In the evening after her work for the state of Michigan was complete, Mary Ellen filled the truck with gas since the fuel gauge didn't work, kept the books, organized, planned and ran her little side business from the dining room table in her home.

She had never run a business before that time. In fact, she had never really dreamed of owning a business. Bit by bit, "Two Men and a Truck" continued to grow and flourish. The United States was in a recession in the 1980's, but Mary Ellen Sheets was not tuned in to the economic forecast. She knew her business provided a valuable service to help people and that demand continued for moving help. "Blind faith" propelled her forward and the learning process, though gradual and painful at times, was overall a great deal of fun mixed in with long hours and a steady focus. "I loved it, and when I couldn't do something big each day, like buying advertising or scheduling a move, I would clean out a file or create a business forecast chart, just to keep doing something each day to move the business forward," she reminisces. For four years, Mary Ellen worked in her Social Services Department office for the state by day and by night, built the foundation for a successful moving company. Through it all, she always managed to find time to volunteer in the community as well.

Finally, the time had come when Mary Ellen wanted to follow her hunch that her side business could support her as her full-time work. Despite the fact that her coworkers thought she was crazy and her mother feared she would "lose everything" she had worked for through the years, Mary Ellen moved forward and took the plunge to quit her "day job". By 1989, her business venture had moved from the dining room table to the basement of her home and later, to a bedroom in the new home she had purchased. The business continued to grow day by day. Within several years, she knew it was time to move to office space outside her home. In 1993, the business officially moved into two upstairs rooms in an old Victorian house in downtown Lansing that had been converted into office space. First two rooms, then three, then eventually the entire house was rented by the "Two Men" organization, including the dirt floor basement space which housed the company's files, a location which the business maintained until their move in 1998 to a 7,000 square foot facility in Okemos, Michigan.

Sally Degnan was the first full-time employee Mary Ellen hired to help with office and administrative responsibilities. Sally was also a single parent mom. Prior to joining the moving company, she was cleaning commercial offices at night and watching other people's children during the day so that she too, could be home during the day with her children. Hers was a difficult schedule at best. Sally's enthusiasm and commitment to help "Two Men" succeed was an asset to the company's growth and gave Mary Ellen a great sense of achievement as she was able to help another person's career growth.

*"I love being able to help others, whether it is my customers, my employees, my franchisees or people in the community. This business has enabled me to give back to other people and that pleases me to be of value in their lives,"* she remarks. Her empathy for other people is one of Mary Ellen's driving forces in her growth as a person and as an entrepreneur. One of her many volunteer experiences early on nurtured this trait of hers. As a volunteer for a crisis hotline, The Listening Ear, she was required to attend a 60-

hour training course in empathy and understanding people's needs and concerns in times of trouble. That training and her volunteer crisis experience proved to be valuable skills in understanding her market, in dealing with business staff and partners and in dealing with customers, particularly when things go wrong. A component of this "empathy training" is now included in the "Two Men" training program for their organization. In a traditional, male-dominated, heavy industry like moving, this personal touch and recognition of people's needs may well be the secret formula that sets this business apart from many others in the same field.

In 1989, another turning point came in the growth of the fledgling business. Mary Ellen, no longer shy and of blushing "Pinkie" status, delivered a speech to a class at the University of Michigan and met another businesswoman presenter, Becky Brevitz, who ran a small successful franchise operation, "The Pet Nanny", offering pet feeding services to vacationing pet owners. Becky encouraged Mary Ellen to talk to the attorney who helped Pet Nanny become a franchise

The rest of the story is history as "Two Men and a Truck International" was born, growing gradually and carefully from that day. In 2000, the franchise organization spanned 22 states with 94 franchise locations completing a total of 140,000 moves annually. Mary Ellen continues her friendship with Becky and is grateful to her for her encouragement to follow this path.

## ▶ A BOTTOM LINE TO BE PROUD OF

The bottom line for both of the moving business entities is impressive as the original Two Men and a Truck operation which still exists today in Lansing, Michigan grossed $2 million in sales last year. The franchise parent company, Two Men and a Truck International, has posted gross sales of $4 to 5 million annually with 30 to 35 employees on staff. It is now the seventh largest mover in the United States.

*"The success of the original moving company is an inspiration to many of our franchise moving companies and serves as a prototype and basis for our training, data systems and marketing,"* reflects Mary Ellen. In 1998, Stick Men University was created and located at the site of the original moving company. This training "university" features a prototype truck, actual furniture and constructed stairways to offer hands-on training in furniture moving techniques and truck loading and unloading, as well as training classes in marketing, customer service and standard reporting procedures that are required of all franchisees. The fiscal fitness of the company's operators is key to maintaining the high standards of the company, so reports and training are used as tools to help operators to learn best practices for the success of their franchise.

Longtime employee, Sally Degnan runs Stick Men University as part of her work at the heart of this growing enterprise. The underlying key to success here is the message to 'treat your customers as if they were your grandparents' and take very special care of them. Extra consideration is always given to customers in highly stressful moves such as after divorce or when moving an elderly person from their own home into a senior citizen residence.

Franchise operators are truly part of something special as they are well informed and rewarded for high achievement even after graduation from Stick Men U. Analysis of their performance rated against their peers provides important guidance as they work as business owners of a franchise in their markets. Leads developed through marketing, referrals, telephone and Internet inquiries are shared by geographic location. Annual meetings offer speakers with the "latest and greatest" needed information and a full course of enthusiasm and positive energy to feed their business appetites. Franchise and employee recognition programs are used liberally to reward the highest performance. An annual top achiever vacation trip and team recognition are incentives for members of the organization to perform well. Top performance is always recognized.

The recent annual meeting theme of "Educate, Motivate, Celebrate" underlies the total approach to this franchise business which respects and recognizes its operators while requiring levels of quality and standard operations in areas the customer can count on when they use a "Two Men" operation. *"We listen to our franchise holders and respect that they work with us as part of our team. It's a balance of their pride in ownership and their entrepreneurship that moves us all to best practices for the company,"* reflects the founder.

Change is a constant as the company has grown. Both of the original 'two men', Mary Ellen's sons, are currently executives in the organization with Brig serving as Franchise Recruiter and Jon as Operator of the original Lansing franchise and Owner/Operator of the Grand Rapids, Michigan franchise. In 1994, Melanie Bergeron, their sister who had opened one of the first franchises in Atlanta, Georgia in 1988, was named company President while Mary Ellen was promoted to Chief Executive Officer. Having her children working together is a terrific experience, although she concedes it is necessary to "depersonalize" business issues that they may disagree upon. As her family and her business are Mary Ellen's two passions in life, there are times when working together requires both personal empathy and balance skills, as any family-based entity would agree. In her own words, *"I am so lucky to have all of my children turn out to be professional business people."*

What's ahead? New "Movers Who Care" software will be standard with all franchise operators soon. Test markets of a Canadian franchise may be in the future for the company. Successful box/carton sales of over one million dollars per year has peaked an interest and test market of a related retail outlet for sales of moving supplies and small freight shipping services. An experiment in the shredding business has ruled out that related enterprise. But a 10 to 15% commercial moving market segment may be a growth area, as will the Internet as it matures, although the company has had a web site for over four years now.

One thing is for sure, Mary Ellen, her family, staff and franchise partners will continue to tune in to the needs and wants of their customers. Everyone who participates in this business will keep their lifeline to this positive energy source where individuals are recognized, creativity and growth are encouraged, and momentum moves forward as they listen and learn from one another and their customers.

## ▶ ROAD MAP TO SUCCESS

This CEO and Founder has been asked why she and her business are now enjoying such widespread recognition including *Entrepreneur* magazine's ranking as one of the Top 500 Franchises in 1993, 1994, 1998 and 1999; Business *Start-Ups* Top 200 Franchises distinction in 1995; the Michigan-Entrepreneur of the

Year award in 1995; Platinum 200 status in 1997 and 1999 issues of *Income Opportunities*; and ranking of Mary Ellen Sheets as #275 in the Top 500 Business Women in *Working Women* magazine in 1999. Her explanation for her recent accolades is simple. *"I started this business helping people and along the way that core value and purpose has stayed the same. It's that simple. Life has a way of giving back to the people who work hard and help others when they do."*

Her favorite saying: *"Do a little every day and you will accomplish a lot."* Sage advice: believe in yourself; work hard; persevere and be honest to achieve success, which she defines as being able to help others with their needs and to help them grow.

New personal developments: about a year and a half ago, Mary Ellen married longtime friend, Tom Amiss. When this charming and confident CEO who has long since shed her early shyness has a moment of free time, you may be fortunate to hear her lecture at a business event in her community or across the country. On the other hand, you may find her in the garden at her new summer home on Lake Huron. Her concluding thought, *"When I look back, I can't believe this all happened. I'll tell you, this country is wonderful!"*

And, according to her friends and staff, so is Mary Ellen Sheets.

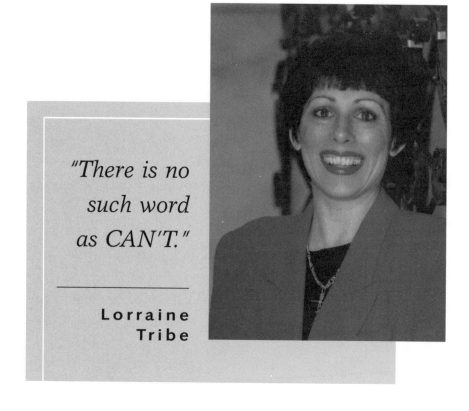

"There is no
such word
as CAN'T."

Lorraine
Tribe

# Quest Personnel (Australia)

Lorraine Tribe wanted to start a business of her own so badly that she sold her home to launch her personnel placement firm. At the time, she didn't realize that one day, she would sell her home again just to keep the business running in hard times.

The story of Lorraine Tribe and Quest Personnel was not

founded in hardship or adversity. Lorraine had been working in the recruiting industry for 10 years as a Senior Recruitment Consultant and Personnel Agency Manager. Life was good. She had achieved senior executive status, was bringing in a handsome six-figure income and had earned the respect of her business associates. By her own admission, she was making a good living and enjoying a comfortable life to the level of that income.

In spite of her existing success, in 1987, Lorraine experienced growing frustration with her work in a highly competitive industry in the Australian business world and abroad, where she saw many questionable business practices were being used. This troubled her. She was convinced that she could drive even greater success with ideas and ethics that were straightforward and would reflect all that she had learned over the years. Lorraine had never really wanted to be a business owner, but as she saw it, this was the only way she could be free to test her conviction that there was a better way to approach her work than in the existing enterprises. She took the leap and decided to go out on her own.

Because she really hadn't saved any money for a business venture like this, the only asset Lorraine had to rely on was her home and property, which were quite lovely and were able to accommodate stables for the horses she owned at the time. Even though it was a difficult choice, Lorraine and her husband went forward with the sale of their home and moved the horses to rented stables in the country. This was the first step in the launch of Quest Personnel.

Lorraine's employer had insisted that she give 12 months notice prior to leaving her executive position. Thinking that this would protect her bonus dollars that were due, she went along with this demand and worked feverishly to clean up commitments for her then employer. Regrettably, the earned bonus never did materialize and little time was available to make advance arrangements for the new business launch.

With little advance planning, there was immediate pressure to get the business on track quickly. Office space, letterhead, phones, marketing plans had to be lined up immediately. (Author's Note: while this Millionaire Woman did not fully launch her business from home initially, later it would move back into the home for a relaunch phase for several years.)

Office space was secured fairly quickly, but there was a delay in the availability of phone lines into the office. It would be four weeks before a phone line could be installed. Good will and good fortune appeared in the face of an elderly tenant across the hall from the new business. This kind neighbor tenant shared his phone with Quest as the telephone was literally pulled into the hallway so that Lorraine could use it in the interim weeks.

## ▶ AN IMMEDIATE HIT

Within 24 hours, Lorraine produced Quest's first job order through cold calling and the business was up and running. Pepsi-Cola was their first client. While they were familiar with Lorraine from her industry experience, they had not been a client of hers up until that time. As a professional courtesy and an example of Lorraine's own principles, she did not bring her previous company's clients with her into the new firm.

Lorraine's early strategy was to target the secretarial and clerical employment markets in both permanent and temporary areas. She felt that by applying an executive recruitment standard of service, she would win clients. The strategy worked and within the first three years major accounts such as State Bank of Victoria, Fosters/IXL and Amcor were added.

With the immediate growth of the business, Lorraine hired staff right from the start. Her first employee would serve as a generalist assuming responsibilities as receptionist, recruiter and placement specialist from the start. This approach to cross-training her associates was a strategy that served the young company well and was maintained as new hires were brought on to staff the growing firm.

Quest expanded. Staff grew quickly and eventually reached 32 members. A move to refurbished premises in Melbourne occurred in 1989. By 1990, just three years after it opened for business, Quest reached over 2 million dollars in sales (the equivalent of 1 million in U.S. dollars according to average exchange rates).

The year 1990 was a roller coaster ride for Quest. Just as they reached new heights in performance, a major recession hit. Many of the new firm's clients were severely affected and were cutting back on use of part-time staff help and recruitment resources in general. Lorraine was caught in the middle of her clients' financial nightmare. As the firm's income dropped dramatically, Lorraine knew she would have to dramatically downsize her staff and cut back on her overhead.

## ▶ *HOME SWEET HOME LOST AGAIN*

Once again, her home had become one of her largest assets and Lorraine had to sell it to pay for incurred operating debts and severance pay for departing personnel. Lorraine's husband, who is an Australian barrister, was able to help negotiate a release from her ten-year lease for commercial office space. Because the economy was in such poor condition, their home was sold for half its original value, but the money was enough to pay off the bills and leave $30 thousand remaining to be used for upcoming business expenses and a home that would serve as Quest's business location as well.

With one employee and little cash available to run a business and buy a home, Lorraine and her husband, Phillip, were starting over in a tough economy. Their choices were limited. They decided to look for a location that was closer to the city since it would serve as both home and office.

A condemned old Victorian home was all they could afford, so they bought it. Although the structure was completely run down and derelict, they believed that over time they could restore it room by room and end up with a convenient location and a valuable property. It took enormous vision and courage to buy the old Victorian place. There was no heating system. It came with a squatter, a homeless gentleman who the Tribe's actually allowed to stay for six months after their arrival until he could be relocated. For most people, it would be difficult to imagine this scenario much less carry on in the midst of such adversity.

By the time they moved in, one large parlor room had been restored and served as the base for the business operation and daytime activities. A newcomer on the scene in their lives by then was the couple's new baby, Stephanie, who also moved into the Victorian house in 1991, along with a nanny to allow Lorraine time to keep the business running. The parlor room was

Stephanie's daytime location as well because it was one of the few rooms with a space heater running to keep the place warm.

Lorraine recalls that several months after they had moved in, they realized that the space heater was really insufficient for the room. She called her brother-in-law, Phillip's brother who is an architect, and pleaded with him that it was so cold that they could not work. He immediately came over with an axe and shovel and broke open an old fireplace that had been boarded up previously. Within two hours, a fire was burning there, and Lorraine, her daughter, nanny, and Quest's one employee could carry on with their daily activities.

At this time, Phillip asked Lorraine why she wanted to continue with this venture? He asked her whether or not it was a good idea to attempt to keep Quest Personnel in operation? In her heart, she knew this was the right course of action. As a mother of a newborn, Lorraine thought it was unlikely that she would find an employer that would allow her the flexibility she would need as a parent and the income level she could realize as a business owner. She was committed to working through the recession years and building for the future with her business. In time, her conviction would prove to be true.

## ❱ PERSISTENCE PAYS OFF

By 1993, business began to look up again as the recession began to lift. That was also the year Lorraine gave birth to her second child, a son, Oliver. Her perseverance and refinement of marketing and sales approaches over the recession years, helped position Quest for rapid growth. By 1994, Quest was fully staffed and moved back into larger commercial office space in East Melbourne. Strategically, the firm had become stronger over the years and was now ready for positioning as a national recruitment service provider serving a broad range of types and sizes of industries.

Lorraine's corporate values that were the foundation for her firm's resurgence are:

- *Ethical dealing*
- *Value for money*
- *Innovation, and*
- *Continuous improvement.*

Quest's clients have observed how the corporate values have carried the firm throughout its emergence. Words that they use to describe Lorraine and her business include: *professional, persistent, tenacious, balanced, innovative, understanding, ethical, adaptable, and client-focused.* Since 1993, Quest has taken off on a growth path with annual revenues exceeding $15 million and gross profit for the firm in the 15% range by 1998. Boeing, Nine West, Ansett and Qantas Airways, Westpac Bank and Midas Mufflers are some of the clients Quest has served.

Over the years, Quest has opened offices in Melbourne (1987), Sydney (1994), Brisbane (1995), Adelaide (1996), Perth (1996), and Hobart (1997) in Australia.

In 1999, Lorraine realized that the business had grown to a size that it needed more working capital if it was going to move up to the next step in the international market. By that time she was also now the mother of three children since the birth of her sons, Oliver in 1993 and Hugh in 1995. From a business and personal standpoint, she thought it was time for a major business partner or perhaps, it was time to be acquired by a larger company. The business would benefit from a stronger capital base. Lorraine would benefit from a situation that would eventually allow her more family time.

A business broker was retained to explore opportunities for a partnership or purchase transaction. Three buyers were identified. Ultimately, on May 5, 2000, Quest Personnel was sold to Skilled Engineering, a $644 million public company recognized as Australia's leading diversified services company with over 10,000 total employees in 60 offices Australia-wide as well as in United Kingdom, New Zealand, New Guinea and Hong Kong. Quest Personnel brought a blue chip, white collar customer base to Skilled Engineering, an organization that was already highly regarded as a provider of supplementary staff for a range of industries including the building and related trades, production, distribution, engineering, technical and drafting arenas.

At the time of the sale, Quest Personnel had reached annual billings of almost $40 million. According to public records as noted in the Skilled Engineering 2000 Annual Report, Quest Personnel was purchased for a combination of cash and stock at a total equivalent value of $4,825,000. Lorraine and Phillip Tribe who were by then both managing Quest, were retained to continue on for five years. That commitment will end in 2005, at which time, Lorraine will enjoy the financial security, flexibility and family time she has worked so hard to achieve since she founded the company.

## ▶ WHEN TO HOLD AND WHEN TO SELL?

Women entrepreneurs today frequently ask their advisors and one another, how do you know when it is time to sell your company? Lorraine Tribe's answer may offer food for thought for other women business owners. *"Knowing when to sell really comes down to an assessment of what you want out of your business experience. A combination of your personal and professional goals and needs must be analyzed to reach a conclusion that is right for a given circumstance."* When Lorraine realized that she had created a huge business organization she asked herself, is this my goal, to run a major business and take it to the next level? Her introspection revealed that what she was really looking for was to replace her traditional $200,000 salary within an ethical, supportive, flexible and creative work environment. Having accomplished this original goal she did not have the passion to sustain the organization of that size for the rest of her life as many other entrepreneurs do.

Lorraine reflected that one of the real challenges of running a company serving major corporations is to maintain performance levels in a high stakes game. *"With contracts of $5 million dollars, it was rewarding to see the company growth, but at the same time daunting to realize that the loss of one or two key pieces of business would have a serious impact on a young firm like ours."*

*"At the highest levels of business performance, it takes greater and greater amounts of resource dollars to keep up with technology that is outdated often within 12 months in a competitive environment. I always knew I wanted to sell my business at some point in time; it had reached a size where it was apparent to me that it needed the financial support of a larger, established parent company."* She adds that, she realized it was a matter of selling at the right time or not selling the company at all.

## ▶ *HOW DID SHE DO IT?*

What were the magic tricks Lorraine used to launch maintain and grow a business amidst such difficult times with 400 competitors in Melbourne alone? How did she motivate her staff to keep going?

The little blue index card file box that Lorraine used to launch Quest Personnel is still with her today. She opened for business with her professional work experience, conviction and the daily newspaper. From the start, she read the paper each day to see who was advertising open positions and approached those companies to help them fill their employee slots. It was as simple and as difficult as that. When companies told her they were not in need of her service, she filed their information in her little blue card box and called them weeks or months later when she saw another need advertised. Professional persistence, logic, service and courage were her hallmarks as she moved into the world of business ownership. *"There's no such word as CAN'T,"* was her motto.

When the business grew, so too did Quest's lead management, database and computer tools. But the basic work was largely the same as they helped companies fill their needs for part-time and full-time employees.

Quest's associates enjoyed the experience of cross training and took part in an active mentoring program in which a seasoned employee helped to train a newcomer in the firm. Job sharing and later, part-time positions helped homemakers get on board the Quest staff, which became known for its emphasis on diversity and personal growth. Respect for associates time and the need for a balanced life were other approaches Lorraine adopted to create a positive work environment. *"We encourage everyone to go home at the end of the day and spend time with their families. Of course there are exceptions that occasionally require long hours on a project. However, there is no special recognition given for staying late routinely, when most days the work can be completed during office hours."*

Her approach to new business development revolved around her strong work ethic, sincere interpersonal skills, and continuous study of the market and the opportunities that presented themselves. *"I found myself asking my clients to just give me a chance to help them. When they did, it was up to me and my staff to offer the best service to meet their needs. If you earn your clients, you keep them."*

Lorraine's belief in innovation and continuous improvement drove her to look for expanding markets and niches Quest could serve. The service of filling secretarial and clerical needs eventually grew to offer a broader spectrum of staffing services including customer service, data entry, technical and telemarketing. In addition to temporary recruitment, the firm went on to offer permanent recruitment, employment consultation, psychological testing, industrial law consultation, Internet services and management reporting.

When asked what role, if any, the Internet has played in Quest's success Lorraine responded that business-to-business electronic commerce is the most significant development to emerge over the past 10 years. She added that a key factor going forward would be to leverage e-commerce media to directly represent your business value set and uniqueness to others. She summed up, *"People-based relationships and performance will continue to be most important in the formula for success."*

### ▶ *DEMONS AND DOUBTS*

Lorraine always had a clear vision of her work and written goals to guide her on her life path. She believed, *"If you don't have written goals, you might not know why you are doing something and where you are going."* In spite of her clarity of purpose, there were key people who made forward progress difficult. Most noteworthy of these were the bankers and accountants she called upon for help early on who were extremely difficult to work with.

*"Banks and accountants treated me like an idiot because I am a woman."* One accountant challenged Lorraine asking how a young girl like her could make so much money and further, that if she could be successful clearly anyone could do this. (He was replaced shortly after this comment.) The lack of respect she encountered was discouraging to Lorraine who did not anticipate this from financial advisors and some clients who preferred to work with men in handling their business. *"I was ignorant of the obstacles starting out, but it was truly more difficult in every way working in the traditional business world as a woman."*

Steadfast in her career purpose, Lorraine became increasingly aware of how the choices she made affected family time needs. She recalls thinking from time to time that it would be enjoyable to be home with the children more and have a slower paced daily routine with them. While she has no regrets and is grateful for her career experience and personal growth, she acknowledges this pull to the home will be satisfied more fully upon her future retirement when she anticipates more time will be available for family and personal pursuits.

Perhaps the only thing Lorraine admits she would have done

differently in retrospect is to find a mentor or network of advisors of her own. *"In hindsight, this would have really helped me because it is so difficult to do it all and think of it all as one individual."* She urges other women in business to find two to three advisors or mentors, whether men or women, who you respect for their intellectual ability. Then, keep in touch with them as you develop your career. *"In recent years, I have met so many fantastic women through professional associations who could have been a great help, particularly early on."*

### ▶ THOUGHTFUL ADVICE

*"Don't be afraid to start something on your own."* Lorraine encourages other would-be women entrepreneurs. She has clearly enjoyed her journey and hopes other women who have a similar vision take the first step and go forward with their plans.

*"So many people I encounter seem to have no clear purpose in their lives. If you have a dream, follow it and don't look back."* Even though Lorraine may opt for a more traditional family role later in life, she feels her decisions helped her to reach the fulfillment of her life work. She believes this is a personal decision everyone must face as they look at their life choices.

Looking back, Lorraine reflects that she is pleased with the success she has achieved through Quest Personnel. The respect of her team and their motivation to contribute and grow is a measure of her own achievement. *"I have watched people grow in their own careers through their Quest experience. I measure my success by the success of my team."*

The Quest Personnel division of Skilled Engineering will continue to be a team to watch over the next four years as Lorraine completes her management contract for her recently sold business. With ethics, value, innovation and continuous improvement as her guiding principles, the story of Lorraine and her contributions to Quest's success will continue to unfold for years to come.

> *"Surround yourself with knowledge and knowledgeable people."*

**Mary Carroll**

# Schoolbelles

It is probably safe to say that Mary Carroll and her Schoolbelles school uniform company have succeeded, in part, because they had God on their side. The bulk of the company's sales, over the past 45 years, have been uniforms for Catholic school students. It's a long story but an amusing one as the feisty and meticulously groomed, white-haired company chairman looks back and shares the details of building a business over many years.

Her career didn't start with uniforms in mind. Mary Miller grew up in Cleveland, Ohio. She attended grade school at Our Lady of Angels and high school at St. Joseph Academy, an all-girls college preparatory academy. She also attended Dyke College in Cleveland. She went on to study fashion and pattern making at Elizabeth Kardos School of Fashion Design, which was located in her hometown. She had learned the basics of being a seamstress from her mother while living at home as a young woman. Design school helped perfect the skills that she used in designing and sewing her own wardrobe. Not long after, Mary took a job in business as a secretary and later, an office manager, learning more about the inner workings of bookkeeping and running a business.

In 1945, Mary was married to Bruce Carroll, who worked in banking at Society for Savings Bank in downtown Cleveland. The Carrolls were avid sailors. Bruce sailed his one design class Star Boat with a racing team out of the Cleveland Yacht Club. With his love for boating, Bruce also built two Star Boats. Bruce and his fellow sailors would come to the Carroll's home to watch the work progress on the boats. Mary would fix late night snacks.

One of the young men, Whitney Miskell, who was a sales representative for George Thomas Sailmakers, was hoping to add a line of foul weather gear to his product line that he sold across the country. When he learned that Mary was an accomplished designer and seamstress, he asked her if she could create and produce such a suit. She agreed to give it a try.

Her dining room table was her cutting table in those days. She made all of her own clothes and those of her two children at the time. She also tailored sports coats for her husband, which he proudly wore with a hand-stitched label that read "Tailored by My Wife." Upon occasion, Mary also sewed for her friends to earn extra income for the family budget.

Once the design of the foul weather gear was complete, Mary needed to find a means to produce it commercially. She thought she might need to take it to New York City, but was unsure of where to start. Bruce suggested that she contact the wife of one of his coworkers at the bank who had a small sewing factory in their same city. Her name was Josephine Rosser. She called her business Kip-Craft, named after her husband, Cliff, whose nickname was Kippy. A meeting was set at Josephine's business, which she had originated in her home in 1955.

At the time, Jo, as she was called, had started her own business making dress up costumes for little girls. This had come about because her daughter liked putting on her mother's beads, high heel shoes, hats and dresses to parade up and down the street. While her "Let's Play Dress Up" costumes were beautifully crafted, there was no easy means to market such a luxury item. FAO Schwartz, the giant national toy company, suggested that Jo revise her products into more marketable lines. Although she was not a Roman Catholic, with that in mind, she altered her plans and created little costumes of nun and priest habits that children could wear at play and at Halloween. The costumes were sold by mail order through two religious goods magazines nationally. In time, she expanded into children's costumes of saints for use at Halloween. These were distributed through the magazines and eventually through religious goods stores locally. Infant of Prague robes and First Communion veils were soon added as they worked to serve the needs of their religious goods distributors.

In 1957, a new opportunity presented itself. One store, Moran's Religious Goods, asked Joe if she could handle an order for green school uniforms for St. Vincent de Paul School, a 300-student order. This was the first break into the school uniform business, which they eventually called "Schoolbelles." Jo took the lead and purchased the needed yardage from a fabric mill in New York City. Next, she needed patterns. She bought a suitable pattern from a Simplicity Pattern Book and proceeded to grade it from size 6 up to size 18. Jo did not have any significant experience in pattern grading which became most evident when the sizing was not correct. Mary was asked to help with the pattern sizing and grading for their first uniform account.

## ▶ SCHOOLBELLES BY KIP-CRAFT

Mary and Jo hit it off immediately and agreed to go into business together on all of their projects. Mary was still working part-time while raising her two young children. In September, the ladies were proud to deliver the beautiful school uniform order on time for the first day of school. By December, however, you could literally read a newspaper through the uniform fabric. The uniforms had worn so badly that they had to replace every one of them free of charge. The fabric mill had no sympathy and no refund for their troubles as Jo had selected a fashion fabric, no one of durable uniform quality. It was a painful lesson to learn early on in the business.

By August of the following year, Jo's financial picture was not good. The women became equal partners when Mary brought new financial resources funded by her mother-in-law for the venture. After the prototype foul weather suit was created and in production, the new partners had great fun working and learning to run a business.

The Kip-Craft team manufactured choir robes, waitress uniforms, and draperies for local motels. They cut pool table covers for a toy manufacturing company in Pittsburgh, hemmed filter for the local gas company, and did anything to keep the business going. Mary reflects, "We were young, vivacious and didn't know that we had a lot to learn. Jo was a redhead and I was a blonde. We talked to everyone we could to learn more about running a business. In the end, we succeeded in spite of ourselves."

Now that they had sold their first uniform account, it was time to go out on their own and secure more school uniform orders. Mary kept talking to her friends and former teachers that she had met while attending Catholic schools in her childhood. The following year, Our Lady of Mt. Carmel Elementary School and eight additional schools signed on for student uniforms.

This time, Mary and Jo set off for New York together to purchase a higher quality grade of uniform fabric. They found just what they were looking for at Deering Milliken Fabric Mill, but the supplier would not sell it to them for the cash they had brought with them to New York. The mill insisted on a line of credit, which the partners did not have or understand. Now that orders had to be filled, the women were in a real bind.

(On a side note, Mary confides that it was a glorious first trip for her to New York City. They walked everywhere to see the sights. She literally wore out the soles and heels of a brand new pair of I. Miller shoes. The ladies stayed at the then famous

McAlpin Hotel, a place where many of the big bands played. It was located at the base of the Empire State Building.)

Disappointed, Jo and Mary returned that cold February to Cleveland without any fabric for the next year's September orders. They decided to approach some of their friends in the industrial fabrics business. Two gentlemen, who owned such a business several blocks from Kip-Craft, agreed to place the order for uniform fabric in return for a charge of interest. The same challenge presented itself when it was time to place an order for white Peter Pan collar blouses. Another gentleman who worked across the street from their factory stepped in and helped the women with a similar arrangement to secure the blouses they needed. In spite of these obstacles, all nine schools were ready on time for school openings.

Mary and Jo had four employees sewing for them. They had a part-time cutter who worked at night. Two of Mary's neighbors helped out packing orders for school delivery. Another dear friend, Mary Ellen O'Boyle, stayed on to become Mary's assistant. She was a faithful and loyal employee. Mary Ellen retired in 1999, but she was always there when needed to help whatever the task.

Schoolbelles, a division of Kip-Craft, was obviously making a name for itself. The following year, an Irish priest from St. Bartholomew's School called and asked the women to make uniforms in a specific red, black and gray plaid patterned material that was the plaid of his family in Ireland. On the annual New York City buying trip, the ladies searched for the exact fabric match to no avail. Their needs were too small to order a custom fabric run, so they made an executive decision and selected another style that had similar colors. There was no time to tell the pastor who was away on vacation that it was not an exact match.

When the uniform orders were delivered for pickup by the parents in the school auditorium after Sunday Mass, the Reverend came running into the room bellowing out "This is not the plaid that I ordered!" It was a low point for Mary, but the school finally accepted the order after Mary explained what had happened. Schoolbelles was off and running and the company's plaid uniform line was launched.

There was still a lot to be learned and painful lessons they were. The following year, the mill did not have any fabric available with the red plaid they had accepted for St. Barth's, so the school uniforms had to be fully replaced once again. This time Mary designed a plaid herself and asked for advance approval of the pastor of St. Bartholomew's parish. He was very understanding when informed of the details of reordering specially made fabrics from the large fabric mills.

Now that the business was growing larger, it was time for Schoolbelles to have a specialty run of fabric for the next year's production. Eventually, the same red plaid fabric became the base of the fabric design for school uniforms that were offered in blue, green, and brown. Today, over 100 colors of the Schoolbelles plaid are available for school selections along with solid colors. All fabrics are available in polyester, gabardine, blends and wool.

Many people wanted to see the business succeed. The families, friends and business associates of the Schoolbelles owners helped out whenever they could. They loaned money and support.

One person who stands out as an early ally is Ronald Cohen, then a young accountant, who offered his professional advice free of charge for the first two years. He told the ladies that he would get paid later when the business became mature. Ron has since retired as the former head of Cohen and Company, a highly successful regional accounting firm. Schoolbelles is a significant paying client of the Cohen firm even to this day. Another friend who also helped with legal matters was their attorney, Tony Viola.

Another noteworthy story of financial assistance involves an episode when the company borrowed $150,000 to buy a business in St. Louis, Missouri that had significant inventory as part of the deal. After a cruel incident when a customer attacked a lone Schoolbelles employee, Mary closed the St. Louis store immediately. Her challenge would be to pay back the loan without the benefit of expansion. Her bank had given her two years to fulfill this obligation. The banker assigned to their account confided that he took the Schoolbelles file with him everywhere, including the rest room, since he was so nervous about the bank examiners possibly thinking this loan was a long shot at best.

Early years were lean years for the business. Mary did not take any salary for the first five years, although she kept a record of her salary so that the company could pay her in later years. It was most important to pay their bills on time and establish a solid reputation for future credit. To date, Mary has not taken this back pay; she explains she liked the feeling of helping out the company financially.

Some times were so tight financially however, that when the landlord, Mr. Johnson of the Johnson Printing Building, would stop by to visit with the women business owners and pick up the monthly rent, on more than one occasion, the ladies would end up delaying the rent and borrowing the payroll from him. He was a great friend and supporter. (The ladies always eventually paid the rent and promised not to tell Mr. Johnson's sons who would not have been pleased at the time.)

By the time that the business had established a reputation and was servicing over 30 schools for girls school uniforms and gym apparel, they moved on to manufacture Schoolbelles' own line of white blouses for girls. In doing so, manufacturing space became limited. At the time, a company across the street from their plant, that produced aprons and daytime dresses, was being offered for sale. This was an ideal facility for production of the new line of blouses.

Again, another financial opportunity arose. Mary and Jo had established a strong relationship with one of their fabric suppliers in New York. The two ladies approached the head executive of the firm for financial assistance in buying the dress factory. He agreed. They now owned another company called "Carmen Lee." Mary helped design dresses and aprons and enjoyed doing so. She went to New York City on many buying trips. This venture lasted for many years. Blouse production grew so large that the plant quit manufacturing aprons and dresses. Eventually, Schoolbelles blouse demand outgrew this plant capacity and the company turned to a manufacturing company in the South to fulfill blouse orders.

Over the years, Schoolbelles moved into sales of boys' school uniforms consisting of pants, dress and knit shirts, jackets, ties, sweaters and socks. The company bought all of these items from subcontractors, except for knit shirts, that they manufactured for a short time. Customer demand again grew beyond company production capabilities. Today, while the company offers a complete line of school uniforms and accessories for boys and girls, the only items manufactured by Schoolbelles are the basic jumper style uniforms, skirts and girls' slacks. The company also does its own monogramming and silk-screening. All school catalogues are printed at Schoolbelles' main office.

After many years of running the business together, Mary and Jo invited their husbands, Bruce and Cliff, to retire from banking and come into the business. They both had served on the company board of trustees and had been helping out whenever needed over the years. Along the way, Jo, who was 15 years older than Mary, and her husband, Cliff decided to get out of the business. They had done very well financially, but were tired of the day-to-day routines. After a six-month sabbatical traveling in Europe, they returned home and asked Mary and Bruce to buy out their share of the business. Jo later spent her time giving talks to senior citizens about her travels in Europe.

As the world of business became more sophisticated, new systems were developed over the years. Mary remembers what a breakthrough it was when they started shipping with United Parcel Service (UPS). She recalls when they first started using credit cards for orders against the advice of many at the time. Family discounts, customized catalogues for every school, bar code shipping, trade shows, computer automation, the opening of retail outlets were all milestones Mary looks back on with great memories and great pride. The arrival of Internet ordering through www.schoolbelles.com has opened even greater vistas for the company's growth that has already expanded to serve close to a thousand schools in 28 states.

Today, 211 associates are employed by Schoolbelles. They serve parochial, private and public school needs for student bodies ranging from six to 2,400 in a school. The full company product line includes school uniforms for boys and girls, athletic and sporting apparel, shirts, sweaters, blouses, accessories, backpacks, jackets, First Communion dresses, socks and the latest addition, a new line of shoes.

Mary's son, Bruce, who worked in the business since he was a teenager, is now president of the company. He remembers and shares stories with his friends about sleeping on the cutting table between rolls of fabrics with his sister, Christine, when they were only five and six-years old. The children rode their bicycles around in the empty areas of the warehouse loft. When Mary took them home after work, they were often covered in warehouse soot.

When Bruce was a young boy he did not want to attend college, but rather focused on learning as much as he could about the uniform business. His practical learning was rounded out by select college courses and seminars he completed to learn more about business management, employee relations, and inventory control. Bruce accompanied his mother on several buying trips from the time he was 19 years old. A highlight of one of their many trips occurred when they returned to a hotel after a long day of buying fabrics to find a telegram that read, "Congratulations Mary! Today your company sales for the year hit $1million!" Mary told her son that one day they would receive another telegram when company sales would grow to $10million in sales. On January 1, 2001, Bruce Jr. sent his parents such a telegram as company sales reached a new milestone since his appointment to president of Schoolbelles. Vice-president, Elaine Stephens, and Bruce Jr. are the senior management team responsible for the business today, while Mary and Bruce Carroll are still kept apprised of major company decisions out of respect for their expertise and founding roles.

In 1999, the company moved from its warehouse district location of over 40 years to a new larger 47,000 location in suburban Cleveland. Currently the company also has stores in Indiana, Illinois and Michigan.

## ▶ PERSONAL MEMORIES

There were few women running a business when Mary was just starting out. She did see many competent women in business when she attended design school and Dyke Business College during the years that her husband was serving in World War II.

Her large Catholic family upbringing was a good training ground for her work ethic and determination to succeed at whatever she undertook, but her career was unconventional for the world at the time. Mary did not ask permission to live her life. She just lived it. A trailblazer, she admits that the demands of her work made it difficult to balance her roles as a wife, mother and businessperson. Somehow, she did the best she could and worked her way through the ups and downs.

In 1960, Mary had a setback in her health. She started to lose her eyesight. Her mother-in-law had died in 1959 and her own mother had recently passed away. At about that same time, Mary and Bruce were to move into their first home, along with their two children and Bruce's father. Mary spent six months in five different hospitals and ended up in the National Institute of Health in Maryland. Throughout this time, Bruce and his father were caring for their two children. Mary eventually returned home without ever knowing what had caused her loss of sight. Today, she only has sight in one eye and maintains enough sight in her right eye to drive a car and play a fairly good game of golf. She is also a colon cancer survivor and thanks God every day of her life.

Looking back, she shares the lessons she has learned that would help other women just starting out.

- *Share the wealth with your employees. Don't be afraid to spend money on bonuses, company parties or employee appreciation days with free lunch and pizza.*
- *Surround yourself with knowledge and knowledgeable people. Ask questions, even if you think you might know the answer.*
- *Being a woman can be an asset, if you are humble enough to let people help you, and if you truly want their help.*
- *Learn from everyone you encounter and remember to thank God every day.*

After 45 years, Schoolbelles is now a $10million company. Mary Carroll and her team have clearly earned an A+ as students of business. The success they have earned must be a reflection that they have learned a lot. Mary and her husband, Bruce, have retired and are living in Florida. They are both in their 70's, in fairly good health, and enjoy golfing as often as they can. Their son, Bruce, and his family are frequent visitors.

> ## "Let's make it happen!"
>
> ### Stephanie Moss

# Solutions Group
## (South Africa)

On a typical work day, you might see Stephanie Moss with her long, dark brown hair pulled back, dressed in light safari clothing, boating down the Orange River under the hot tropical sun. Or perhaps you will see her and a guide in a rubber dinghy, white-water rafting with corporate clients on the Zambezi River. Whether running a travel incentive, a new product launch, a special event, or team building session, Stephanie Moss has spent countless days in the land of elephants, rhinos, lions and giraffes. The zebras, leopards, cheetahs and ostriches most of the world only view in captive environments run freely in Stephanie's native land. Her work as the founder of Solutions Group event planning firm has zeroed in on the magnificent environment of her continent.

The evolution of the Solutions Group began in 1989 in Johannesburg, South Africa. At that time, Stephanie Moss was 25 years old. Her career work since graduating from business college with a diploma in general business included experience in administrative work at an advertising agency, eventual account executive responsibilities, and promotion to marketing manager for an accounting firm in United Kingdom, where she lived for two years. Upon returning to South Africa in 1987, Stephanie landed a marketing position with Unisys, the international computer corporate giant.

In her brief, fast track career, Stephanie had learned much about marketing, advertising, promotion and special event management. She had worked on numerous major projects and had learned the ropes and business basics in the field. At the same time, she was growing discontent with working for large companies. She often felt like she was "just a number" in such large organizations. By age 25, Stephanie wanted to strike out on her own and create her own business for the future of her career.

While still working for Unisys, she spent her evenings at home planning what her next step in starting a company would be. She decided to build on what she knew and to go out on her own as an event planner. Fortunately, she was able to share a portion of office space within a small graphic design firm that she had used as a corporate client; their office was located within a ten-minute drive of her home. A shared secretary would give the upstart company the appearance of being larger. The rent was modest and so Stephanie signed on.

With no clients and no real capital investment, she knew that it was critical that she find business right away. Armed with the yellow pages directory and a telephone, she began with the letter "A" section and scanned the pages for companies that were well known or looked large enough to need her services. That first week she spent each entire day calling prospects by telephone and sharing her capabilities for their business needs. By the end of the week, she secured her first client, a businessperson who knew her from her work in the information technology industry. Soon, second and third assignments were lined up and Solutions Group was officially in business assisting in organizing conventions, special events, product launches and travel incentives.

Within about eight months, Stephanie added staff, a part-time person to assist with the administrative work of running the business. After the business was a little over a year old, a full-time sales person was also added, leaving Stephanie open to organize, plan, and service the assignments for special events that were now on schedule. Shortly after, the young business moved into larger office space and a special events co-ordinator was hired to assist with the many details of client work.

Within three years, the firm had continued to grow gradually and had a staff of five full-time people. After renting office space for the first four years, Stephanie decided to move the business into her home and purchased a beautiful, large home in Hyde

Park, an area that was considered by many to be one of the best suburbs of Johannesburg. It occurred to her that she would rather be paying rent to herself than to a landlord. The home she purchased had a separate entrance for the offices, which were attached to the main house. This decision to move Solutions Group into Stephanie's home would reap big rewards later, as the property appreciated in value and was a profitable investment over time.

Six years after the company was founded, Solutions Group reached $1 million in sales. In a business that sells time and services, this was a considerable achievement. Today, the firm is fully staffed with ten highly experienced women associates. Annual billing in year 2000 was just under $4 million. Late last year, Stephanie purchased a larger property with two structures, a home and an office facility, and moved her company to an even more handsome "home" office.

## ▶ BLUE CHIP SERVICE

Solutions Group has developed a blue chip list of local and international clients. Novartis Pharmaceuticals, Glaxo Wellcome, Phillips, Microsoft, Siemens, Toyota, Mercedes Benz, City Bank, Aspen Pharmacare, Unisys, and MSD (Merck) are among the companies that they have served while becoming one of South Africa's major event management companies.

Key components of a Solutions Group assignment include strategic planning for creative event themes, travel arrangements, accommodations, audio visual presentations, promotional materials, itineraries, banquets, entertainment, tours and budgets. The firm offers to "take the strain and do all the work" for clients who are looking for venues and meetings "of quality and character".

*"Do it right or don't do it at all,"* is the motto Stephanie lives by in her business. Doing it "right" for her blue chip clients can be particularly challenging working in a country that has undergone much unrest and civil strife in recent memory. The location of safari style trips has to be carefully researched and monitored for the current civil situation. Local guides are always needed for trips through the bush and local customs dictate what dignitaries expect as gifts or a token of appreciation from visiting travelers. Stephanie and her staff are masterful at keeping a pulse on all of these developments, while tending to the business details of running successful business meetings and events.

*"It's up to us to make the event experience as comfortable and memorable as possible for our clients. We call upon our creativity and attention to detail to take care of even the smallest aspect of the overall event."*

## ▶ PERSONAL SOLUTIONS, PERSONAL SUPPORT

Stephanie's usual positive thinking is seasoned with realism as she reflects on the many obstacles that she has encountered along the path to building her business. One of the most challenging of these was the attitude of many of the marketing decision-makers who were potential buyers of her service. She found that particularly middle-aged men were taken back by a 25 year old woman who presented her company in a very strong manner as the remedy for their special event management needs. Her response was to *"never give up." "I was thick-skinned and tenacious and wouldn't take it personally if they said no to me at the first point of contact."*

Burnout is another challenge many event planners face. Stephanie explained that when she found that she and her staff were overwhelmed in fulfilling a heavy schedule of commitments, her solution was to carefully organize and prioritize the work, and as soon as feasible to take a day or two off and restore their energy level. On some occasions, this was an indication that it was time to add staff and Stephanie did so. (As an aside she mentioned that several times she has also taken members of her staff on a weekend of rest and relaxation to such destinations as Milan or Amsterdam.)

## ▶ SUPPORTS TO SUCCESS

Stephanie's father was a great support to her when she started the business. He took her to meet with his attorney and his accountant to ask their advice in the early startup period. While the actual meetings did not uncover any major changes that Stephanie can recall, she remembers fondly her parents' support.

Early on her associates at the graphic design firm she rented space from were big supporters of Stephanie's venture. Friends encouraged her over the years as well. While her first marriage ended after three years, her then husband did support her and understood the pressure of starting up a new enterprise. A number of years after her divorce, Stephanie remarried a gentleman she met in her work as an event planner.

Bruno was managing East African hotels, based in Nairobi, Kenya when Stephanie met him. She had traveled there for advance planning of a convention that would be held at his facility. After 18 months, Bruno moved back to his native South Africa and he and Stephanie were married. Recently, the couple welcomed their first child, a daughter, who reaps the benefits of her mother's home office location and the extra time it affords for time together.

When asked if her entrepreneurism had made an impact on her personal life, Stephanie replies that it was the path to meet her current husband and begin a family. She is looking forward to enjoying this new chapter in her life.

## ▶ BUSINESS REFLECTIONS

While Solutions Group has matured and grown along side its major advertising agency competitors, the business climate has changed in South Africa. Strife within the country has escalated at times over the years. Currently, Stephanie reflects that a white woman-owned business is now at a disadvantage in some ways, because of the black economic empowerment policies put in place by the South African government and expected by corporations of their suppliers over the past three years.

More challenging yet is the fact that hundreds of people claim to be in the event management business today in South Africa and surrounding markets. Keeping Solutions Group's work high profile requires constant vigilance and energy. *"Creativity and teamwork are the talents we are called on to create new solutions, new approaches"*. When a great idea comes to her in the evening, Stephanie keeps a little black book next to her bed and makes a quick note.

Steady networking is another approach that has worked well

over the years for business growth. *"Even after 11 years in business, I still love entertaining, socializing and creating memorable events for guests. I am not afraid to offer someone my card at a social gathering. It takes that persistence and self-confidence to keep the momentum going."*

The Solutions Group staff is a highly talented team of professionals with impressive track records in event management and hospitality as well. They know that Stephanie's challenge to them is *"Let's make it happen!"* The diversity of their work and the adrenaline rush associated with creating impressive major events has kept this busy staff in focus and growing. Their founder has great respect for the many talents they bring to the team. She prefers to hire women because her experience has shown their attention to detail is greater for event management work.

## ▶ HEROES, ROLE MODELS & ADVICE

Margaret Thatcher, former prime minister of England, is one of Stephanie's heroes in life. *"She is unbelievable in her achievements."* She also respects and admires Chris Patton who was the last governor of Hong Kong Island.

While Stephanie claims to have no active mentors, she mentioned that several women she worked with early on in her career did have an impact on her growth and personal vision. One was a woman executive who she worked for at the advertising agency in the United Kingdom. There was also a woman at Unisys who had sold her own business to that corporation previously. Both of these strong, successful women inspired and taught Stephanie much about business and life by their example.

If there was one thing she would have liked to do differently so far, she remarked that she wished she had taken on a larger scale goal from the start. Even though the company has grown every year and has already done international work, in retrospect, Stephanie sees it has great potential to be even larger and may consider acquiring another smaller firm in the future. Recently, she was approached by a major travel agency to consider a merger, but declined the offer for the current time.

Her advice to other women considering starting a business of their own: *"Have clear and focused goals and know what is driving you. Be tenacious. Never give up. Give it 110%."* What she appreciates most from her own business journey is the *"sense of independence, power and control over your own destiny."*

She recommends that women consider joining a professional women's association to find a support network for their ideas. However, to date, she still finds that mixed business associations of men and women tend to include more of the decision makers who could be future clients for her business.

While she is passionate about her enjoyment of her work, Stephanie is less so about her personal fitness routine. She disciplines herself nevertheless to schedule time each week for jogging, weight training and cardiovascular workouts. *"In the midst of your busy life, it is critical that you take care of yourself. After all, your health is the foundation of your success."*

Stephanie Moss' success with Solutions Group will continue to be a work in process. Her story is a testimonial to the emergence of women entrepreneurs on the business scene throughout the developing countries of the world. If a woman can build a thriving business on a service that organizes regular canoe trips in Africa and piranha fishing in the Amazon jungle for executives, anything is possible in the highly competitive, "shark-infested" world waters of our contemporary business environment.

# Success Secrets

# CLUSTER THREE—
# *Momentum*

▶ *SUCCESS SECRET #9: Business Savvy*

**The Internet, Franchise, Investments**

## The Internet

The Success Secrets included in this chapter deal with more sophisticated business plan areas including the Internet, franchise opportunities and savings for the future. The first of these focal points is the Internet.

Any consideration of Success Secrets would not be complete without mention of the role of the Internet in business success as experienced by the sixteen successful women profiled in this book. While the "dot.com explosion" of the 1990's has come and gone, the Internet continues to be a driving force of change in our world and in the way we do business. According to Forrester, a leading independent emerging technology research firm, nearly 20 million households shopped online in December, 2001, spending an average of $304 per person. By their reports, total online sales for 2001 reached $47.6 billion. Some analysts predict that U.S. e-commerce will reach $4.8 trillion in transaction value by 2004.

With all this online commerce, what has been the experience of the Millionaire Women? All of the women profiled in this book have a business web site and communicate by e- mail. The Internet was typically not the first business consideration these entrepreneurs shared, however, it was definitely in the mix. Because these companies were not born as primarily "dotcom" businesses, for the most part, they have used the Net as a marketing tool or an extension of their distribution channel.

Gun Denhart of HannaAndersson shares that relatively early on, the Internet accounted for over 20% of her sales of children's soft, durable clothing sold primarily by catalogue through direct mail. The Internet was a boost to the core business tactics already in place and it served to help develop the Japanese market for HannaAndersson. Lillian Vernon has also made her catalogue line available online and offers personalized products, special sales and help with gift ideas.

Doris Christopher of The Pampered Chef takes her Internet sales and marketing strategy one step further and offers a bridal gift registry through www.pamperedchef.com. Giftware and kitchen products are mailed directly. Orders are taken 24 hours a day, seven days a week.

Schoolbelles, founded by Mary Carroll, offers online purchase of their complete line of school uniforms and accessories. Orders can be placed at www.schoolbelles.com and later visited again to check the status of shipping and delivery.

The founders of Vera Bradley and Cookie Bouquet use the Internet to showcase their products and help customers find a retail store in their community. Both of these companies use a Store Locator reference page to make it easy for customers to make an in-person retail purchase. While customers currently cannot order online directly, they can view web pages complete with features and colorful illustrations of many items.

Rian van Velzen-Bastiaansen of Nature's Choice uses her Internet site for illustration purposes only for her business-to-business customers who are interested in her line of personal care and comfort goods. Barbara

Mowat uses her business-to-business site as a marketing tool and an enrollment mechanism for readers to subscribe to her *Home Business Report.*

Clearly there are many ways to include the Internet as a component of a business as evidenced by the different approaches shared here and in the other Millionaire Women success paths. However, there are a few rules of thumb to consider when developing a strategy or approach. Words of wisdom in this arena have been shared by cleveland.com, a premiere news website affiliated with *The Plain Dealer* daily newspaper and by Acero, Inc. a strategic consulting and solutions provider. Their expert advice on Internet strategy and use follows here.

What the Internet can do effectively is serve as a communications tool. This can be a great source of networking for a home-based business as a resource and a forum to exchange ideas with others in a similar line of work. In addition, the Web can be leveraged as a communications tool in many ways including:

- Product Research
- Competitive Intelligence
- Marketing/Advertising
- Direct Sales
- Customer Service
- Value-Added Services and
- E-mail.

Product research and competitive intelligence gathering are fundamental to the launch of a new business in the development of a core business plan. Online access to statistical information and web sites of potential competitors is a real advantage in business planning and ongoing strategy.

Marketing and advertising are among the most visible Internet applications as seen on individual business web sites as well as on related links or publications. Many have effectively used this approach to create added visibility for a company or product or to create an image that may help a business appear larger or more successful than it may actually be. It can offer linkage to a local customer base along with new opportunities and larger global markets. An attractive and effective web site can help to drive business and overall sales.

In consideration of e-commerce, the Internet can serve as a direct sales mechanism to expand existing sales channels or fill in this role, particularly for a young company with budget limitations on hiring staff. The 24/7 feature of online sales is also appealing to keep sales in the pipeline at all times. Customer service and value-added applications are additional features and functionality that may be of value to help meet business needs.

E-mail, which is one of the most visible outcomes of the Internet, is another tool for communication that can save time and money for a business owner. Communication is really the core process delivered by the Web.

As any communication tool, the most effective applications have clearly paid attention to the basics. Attractive graphics, sound copywriting, and good headlines are at the heart of success here. If the goal is to build brand awareness and ultimately drive sales, Web pages need to be well designed to meet those needs. Young companies are encouraged to secure a domain name and establish at least a rudimentary web page, as it is important that they begin the process early on. Consultants can help move the evolution of the communication online, but the process has to begin somewhere. While basic design can get a business started, professional help will typically help secure the best outcome.

Other words of wisdom from the online specialists urge businesses to pursue strong positioning through available search engines like Yahoo and Excite. Location is everything when searching key links to a site.

Once a web site is up and running there are few things to always keep in mind. First, having a web site is not a substitute for having a marketing plan. This is just one element of an overall sales and marketing strategy. It is the rare company that will survive long-term with web marketing as its only approach, as is evidenced by the "dotcom demise" of recent years. Work will be needed to drive people to a web site and to keep them coming back for another positive experience.

A final word: no matter what happens, test the results that any web page offer or activity yields. Web marketing is dynamic and evolving and requires careful attention for best results.

## Franchise

It is possible that many of these success stories would have taken place without a strong distribution system, but it is unlikely. In fact, the distribution channel for many of the Millionaire Women's products was at the core of their success. Discovery Toys, Mary Kay Cosmetics, and The Pampered Chef opened doors and created opportunities for women in business who have sold their products with enthusiasm through home shows and direct sales to the consumer. Other noteworthy businesses not featured in this collection include Tupperware and The Longaberger Basket Company. The beauty of this approach is not only the wide talent pool from which sales agents can be drawn, but also the economy of creating a commissioned sales force that is compensated directly and proportionately out of profits.

Another method of distributing a product, while building a large regional, national or international company is franchising. Mary Ellen Sheets became familiar with the potential of franchise business through a friend who encouraged her to consider it. The accelerated growth of Two Men and a Truck resulted. By sharing a common concept and spreading out the financial burden for running a large regional or national entity, an entrepreneur can speed up her timeframe for organizational growth and create momentum not possible without a franchise organization. Gwen Willhite had a similar story to tell about how crucial the franchise process has been to the growth rate of Cookie Bouquet and Cookies By Design market penetration. Both Gwen and Mary Ellen now have sophisticated business plans that include franchise product, systems and quality training along with franchise performance recognition programs. There are business lessons to be learned in the franchise area to maximize the approach for a would-be entrepreneur starting a franchise. The gains and the flexibility for a young company are worth exploring if this is the distribution system that makes sense.

Ample information is available today through professional business associations for franchisors and franchisees. The International Franchise Association (www.franchise.org) appears to be the most comprehensive of these resource groups with information available on franchise opportunities, programs, services, news, political action, technology and tutorials on how to create a franchise organization. In 2001, they hosted their 42nd Annual International Franchise Convention for members and prospects. International and women-related franchise information are also offered through this association. Their Women's Franchise Committee (WFC) formed in 1996 is dedicated to encouraging women in franchising through an international network and educational programming.

The American Franchisee Association (www.franchisee.org) is another resource to consider in the franchise area. This organization was formed in 1992 to improve business conditions for franchising generally, while working to protect business interests of franchisees. Depending upon whether a person is considering becoming a franchisor or franchisee, this may be an association worth exploring.

From the view of a woman considering starting a business of her own, a position as a full commissioned sales representative, like those mentioned previously, or a franchise opportunity may provide the venue to launch a new business, particularly if she has an interest in working from home. In essence, Mary Kay Cosmetics' leader, Arlene Lenarz, had the best of both worlds as a representative of the renowned beauty line. She was able to be an entrepreneur in her own right while enjoying the strength, brand name and stability of a major corporation, which incidentally had been founded years previous by a woman working from home. Arlene is running her own very successful business while in the larger framework of the Mary Kay organization.

In short, "consider franchise" when building a business plan is a success secret that has brought significant rewards to many.

## Investments

While most new businesses will channel the majority of their financial resources into the operations of a young venture, sooner or later, consideration of investing in the future will likely become an issue. Once companies begin to grow and generate profits, financial investments, particularly in the area of retirement planning typically arise.

A recognized expert in the area of employee benefit arrangements shares that while many young entrepreneurial companies start out directing the bulk of their profit back into the business, some will establish qualified retirement plans for employees and themselves. Frequently, the plans of young companies are funded only by employee's salary deferrals under a 401K plan to save for their retirement and defer income tax.

Once companies become more established and begin to generate consistent profits along with needed operating revenue, the owner can improve its 401K plan to include an employer matching contribution. A low cost plan like this might feature an employer contribution of $.25 on each dollar of employee 401K savings up to an amount equal to 4% to 6% of total pay. This type of arrangement results in a cost to the employer of about 1% to 1.5 % of payroll.

As businesses mature, stabilize and grow, so too will their employee benefit arrangements as is evidenced by the sophisticated array of such plans used by businesses today. Wide variations are available on plan strategy and design, depending upon the desired goals. More generous plans can be designed so that the employer contributes 15% or more of payroll. Generous employee benefit plans may serve as a recruitment or retention tool. Other plan designs can be created to provide minimal employer cash outlays for the rank and file employees, while maximizing plan contributions for owners to create a personal tax shelter.

Whether plans favor employee or employer contribution, all tax-qualified retirement plans are strategically valuable in planning for the future with savings that are protected from personal and corporate creditors in the possible event of a downturn in the business.

What is key to making any short-term or long-term financial plan work is good counsel. Many Millionaire Women turned to mentors or experts for financial ideas, while others operated more intuitively with their financial planning. In retrospect, however, the majority agreed that trusted, informed advisors in the finance and investment arena were well worth the fees incurred in creating a sound plan, as long as the company founders remain involved in the planning, implementation and tracking.

## ▶ SUCCESS SECRET #10: Help Others Succeed

California-based author and lecturer, Mel Kaufmann, best known for his *Millionaire Handbook* of ideas geared to assist in the pursuit of millionaire status, holds forth that, "The open hand of giving is never empty." It is his position that in giving to others, good fortune returns to the giver, if not immediately then in indirect ways. Mr. Kaufmann's philosophy holds true for the experience of the Millionaire Women.

Early hires in many of the profiled organizations were individuals who grew and developed their business skills along side the owner of the company. Often these people stayed on for many years and rose through the ranks in responsibility and stature. The opportunity for success in these instances was shared by the entrepreneur with her associates.

Loyalty of employees is ultimately seen in the low turnover rates of these firms. Social gatherings, recognition programs and flexible benefits are staples of many of the Millionaire Women companies. Lillian Vernon and Mary Carroll of Schoolbelles mastered the art of employee recognition and respect years ago. In South Africa, Solutions Group owner, Stephanie Moss, has taken her key staff members on weekend getaways as a reward for long hours and superior performance.

Margaret Johnsson of The Johnsson Group of financial consultants has perhaps the most forward-thinking employee giveback as she insists that her consulting staff take a company-paid two-week travel sabbatical after three years working with her firm. Margaret approves proposed plans and offers $1000 spending money along with the paid time off. She holds that creativity and "breakthrough ideas" can best be nurtured by encouraging associates to step away from the daily routine and look for creative solutions to client needs and service.

Helping others succeed is a recurring theme in conversations with all of the Millionaire Women. Whether considering employees, suppliers and vendors, customers or the community, these successful women are committed to giving something back. Barbara Mowat of "Uniquely Canada" and *The Home Based Business Report* has built her entire business around the company's mission of helping small businesses bring their products to market. Cynthia Jones of Jones Worley Design shares her knowledge and inspiration as a lecturer within her community and at key speaking engagements.

Philanthropy is another path many have chosen as a means to help others. Gun Denhart's nationally recognized program of recycling and donating clothing, dubbed "Hannadowns", for needy children is truly noteworthy. Vera Bradley Designs' creation and support of the Vera Bradley Golf and Tennis Classic fundraiser for breast cancer research is another outstanding example of community support. The Pampered Chef and others offer product shows to support select non-profit entities.

The many approaches to helping others succeed circle back to Arlene Lenarz of Mary Kay Cosmetics remarks on the "Law of the Universe: the giver is truly the receiver."

## ▶ *SUCCESS SECRET#11: Relationships are Everything*

The level and appreciation and attention to relationships with staff, customers and vendors, exhibited by the Millionaire Women is much higher than that evidenced in many businesses today. "Relationships are everything," is a mantra heard over and over in conversations with this high-performing group of women entrepreneurs. This is obvious in the way they treat their human resources with careful hiring, frequent recognition, teamwork and celebration of success. Mary Carroll of Schoolbelles echoes a common feeling, *"Don't be afraid to spend money on bonuses, company parties or employee recognition."*

Schoolbelles' early success was also enabled on several occasions by the founders' relationships with larger clothing manufacturers and a major accounting firm that assisted them in early buying and finance. Relationships with suppliers can be a real asset in running an effective business. This relationship theme of the Millionaire Women runs throughout their interaction with employees, customers, suppliers and loved ones.

Mary Ellen Sheets' Two Men and a Truck success strategy revolves around the highest levels of empathy and respect for her associates and her customers in the transportation industry, one not usually typified by a warm and caring style. She encourages her staff and franchise associates to "treat customers as if they were your grandparents and take very special care of them."

It is obvious that money does not, in fact, buy everything even at highest levels of achievement. Good relationships are a focus and goal at every level for the Millionaire Women. This human resource or relationship emphasis, however, appears to be a success secret that is integral to the company's mission and corporate culture. It is genuine or it doesn't work. Realizing that sincerity and integrity are companions to this approach is another success secret in its own right.

## ▶ SUCCESS SECRET #12:
## Write Down Your Goals and Dreams

In a study of 1953 Yale University graduates, factors that effected lifetime success were evaluated. After reviewing such variables as intelligence quotient, academic performance and others, it was determined that the most successful graduates had one thing in common, written goals. This powerful tool has not been lost on the Millionaire Women.

Lorraine Tribe of Quest Personnel in Australia believes, *"If you don't have written goals, you might not know why you are doing something and where you are going."* She adds, *"So many people I encounter seem to have no clear purpose in life."* Written goals may be the antidote to the fuzzy thinking Lorraine describes.

Lillian Vernon concurs: *"Have a business plan and follow it."* As Arlene Lenarz of Mary Kay Cosmetics puts it, *"Success is a daily progression toward a worthwhile goal."* Margaret Johnnson, who keeps a "dream board" of written goals in her personal computer files, encourages, *"Write down your dreams."*

While every successful woman in this collection of profiles did not have written goals, many did. All of these entrepreneurs had clear goals and objectives for their work. If the Yale University study findings hold true, those that wrote down their goals and dreams may have enjoyed more clarity if not more success than their counterparts. In any case, it is a secret many shared that should be considered by anyone modeling after their success.

> *"Most people are not successful because they are not willing to suffer for success."*

**Cynthia R. Jones**

# Jones Worley

Cynthia Jones is a petite, young African-American woman who took an obstacle that could have seemed insurmountable and turned it into an opportunity. In 1990, she was an unlikely candidate to start a business having worked in the predominantly, white, male-dominated architectural design/ construction industry in Atlanta, Georgia. But Cynthia had a good mind for business, a strong background in communications and graphic design, and a vision to own a company one day. Twelve successful years later, it appears that her analysis of a niche market for a woman and a minority was right on track.

When Cynthia graduated from Georgia State University in 1984 with a bachelor of visual arts degree in graphic design, she was enthusiastic about the start of her career. She immediately started work for Stevens & Wilkinson, a majority-owned architectural firm, and several years later, signed on with the minority-owned Turner & Associates architects and planners. In both of these firms, she learned the management of design services and the process for marketing to architects and developers who utilized large-scale environmental graphics on their projects.

Cynthia had her first entrepreneurial experience at the early age of 15 when she sold five of her acrylic paintings to her high school teachers and friends. In college, she worked as a freelancer, designing logos and publication layouts for her professors and start-up companies. Then in 1988, she joined several male business associates in a new venture that would focus on displaying public health messages on small billboard-like signs in large, high traffic public facilities. She was intrigued with the idea and agreed to lead the initiative. To support herself, she provided design consulting to both of her former architectural employers on various assignments and for several new clients that she had acquired. The public health messages concept turned out to be a great idea, but one that was ahead of its time as it lacked sufficient support for its success. After two years, Cynthia refocused her time on her design-consulting career that had been steadily growing and providing her an encouraging income.

While consulting, Cynthia would often hire one of her former coworkers at Stevens & Wilkinson, Barry K. Worley, to assist her on assignments. In the fall of 1989, Cynthia and Barry discussed whether or not they should pool their resources and talents to start a business together. Cynthia was clearly bringing in more work than she could handle herself. Over the next few months, they explored the idea and came up with a business plan that had terrific potential.

In their business plan analysis, Barry and Cynthia discussed the fact that, at that time, there were no women and minorities providing signage to architectural and construction firms, many of which had government standards for participation. Cynthia knew that their combined talents, diverse experience, gender difference and racial makeup would position them as a strong new team in the industry. Cynthia would have responsibility for business development, operations and the firm's finances. Barry, who had earned a degree in industrial design in college, would be the principal in charge of project work. They agreed that they would both participate in the firm's core business of design to ensure quality and excellence.

Since Cynthia had begun the business in her home, had brought to the new venture revenues from her existing corporate clients, and had created the vision for building the organization and its unlimited potential, she maintained majority ownership. A deal was struck, with Cynthia at 65% ownership and Barry owning 35%, and Jones Worley was up and running. There was a strong mix of personality and style with an African-American woman and a white male as business associates at the helm of this dynamic new enterprise. Cynthia remarks that she was comfortable with this arrangement and that the corporate structure was right for the business/political climate.

She knew that a partner relationship with Barry would be successful and that her ownership shares would support her leadership and role as president and chief executive officer of the organization. She also knew that every experience she had leading up to this had prepared her and allowed her the personal and professional growth needed to make the hard decisions that would lie ahead.

The two shareholders of Jones Worley pulled together a total of $1,250 to open an account with a bank for the new business. Their contributions were in proportion to their ownership shares, plus Cynthia threw in an additional $250. It would be the only personal investment that would be needed to launch the business. From their very first day together, each month's revenues determined salaries and expenses. For twelve years, the firm primarily operated on revenues and a modest line of credit. The company has never relied on outside capital.

## ▶ UP AND RUNNING STRONG

It didn't take long for growth to come. It was clear almost immediately that they would need to move out of Cynthia's home studio into commercial office space. First a two-room, then three, then four-rooms of office space were rented by Jones Worley. Within six months, the firm moved to a new building for more growing room. Six years later, the principals decided to buy a circa 1910, two-story 5,000 square foot mansion in midtown Atlanta that had formerly been the home of the American Lung Association for more than fifty years. Its beautiful original design was renovated five years ago by the design firm and it is the place they call home to the business today.

As staff numbers and capabilities grew, so too did receivables. By the end of the fourth year, the young firm had reached more than $1 million in annual sales. (A record of current annual billing remains confidential. Cynthia firmly believes that public financial disclosures are not appropriate for the privately held company. Every year the company's billings have grown and the enterprise has been profitable.) She reflects, *"Nothing is served by flaunting numbers except to satisfy others' curiosity. We work to advance our firm every year and measure our success within the partnership."* She goes on to encourage everyone to find their own purpose in life and remain steadfast without comparing their achievements to the success of other people. *"If an apple compares itself to an orange it will always be unhappy . . . if being an orange is the goal."*

In addition to large, outdoor, environmental graphics, the firm offers a comprehensive range of communications graphic design services including corporate identity programs, corporate collateral development, video production, and web site design. Jones Worley currently employs 16 people and has completed work on over 200 major projects in more than 50 cities throughout the United States, along with assignments in the U.S. Virgin Islands, Switzerland, Denmark, Hawaii, and Indonesia. Their portfolio includes major sign systems for no less than ten airports, twelve stadiums and numerous hospitals and educational institutions. (Visitors encountered the firm's work in the 1996 Olympic Games in Atlanta, Georgia at more than seven Olympic stadiums and venues.) Growth has been progressive and continues to be well managed as the business evolved from its early days to providing a broader scope of services in a larger geographic market.

The firm's vision as set forth by the partners from the outset is "to advance the firm and serve as one of the country's leading design organizations which attracts and maintains notable clientele and highly skilled, motivated professionals, while creating a profitable and enjoyable work environment." Cynthia was not sure that the world was ready for her vision or her unconventional partnership when she launched it in 1990. Time would show that the quality of her team's work would compete well in the commercial market while she moved into a niche that had formerly not been served.

## ▶ THE JOURNEY OF BUSINESS AND LIFE

This year, as the firm celebrates its 12th anniversary and Cynthia turns 40 years old she looks back at the journey thus far. When asked if her gender has been an obstacle or an asset her answer is "both". Although I have worked for quite a while in a male- dominated industry, the world is looking for more minority-owned and female-owned businesses. With regard to her clients and her staff, she remarks that as a leader, it is important that you command the respect of your closest associates. *"You must insist on their respect. Their loyalty is something that you earn."*

Her definition of an obstacle is her favorite quote: *"Obstacles are those frightful things you see when you take your eye off your goal. Deal with them and find others who share your vision."*

She defines success in life and business as *a journey, not a place. "To me, every blessing I have had, every accomplishment I have achieved is for learning and sharing with others."*

Spiritual by nature and by choice, Cynthia calls upon her belief in the divine to carry her through difficult times. *"My prayers are simple. I thank you god for sight, for breathing, for grace, for his blessings and for the love of my family and friends. I ask him to cover my decisions personally and professionally. And where I encounter hardship and pain, I pray for faith and strength to bear my crosses.*

For her, there are no bad days, just bad moments in the day. Now, Cynthia acknowledges as she has grown wiser in her adult years how important the moment is in any given magnificent day.

## ▶ A GREAT FAMILY TREE

Cynthia's success does not surprise her family, even though they did not always understand the choices she was making from time to time. Her large, close-knit family includes her three sisters and father and a wide array of extended aunts, uncles, cousins and the like. (Sadly, her mother passed away of diabetic complications when Cynthia was just 23 years old.) Cynthia describes her family as extremely close with a lifetime of memories together having fun and grieving family losses. Her family has been one of her greatest sources of strength and support.

Even as a child Cynthia always knew that she wanted to lead something in her adult life. Her sisters and cousins knew that if they were playing school Cynthia, although the youngest, always had to be the teacher or she wouldn't play. While in high school, she found a way to take college classes at a local university. Her siblings watched her take two buses and a train to get there. Upon high school graduation, she was the only black student who was an honors graduate. Early on in life, she decided that education was her link to her life's success. *"We all have to plant the seed that allows success to grow."*

Cynthia Jones is passionate about her life and her career in every way. In fact, she feels so strongly about it that she is often asked to lecture to women, business and student groups to share her vision and inspiration.

As she grew older and started her career journey, she found great comfort in visiting her grandparents and just enjoying their company. *"We didn't talk about anything in particular on those visits; I just enjoyed their company and their unconditional love and support."*

Her great uncle, Dr. Major Jones, was president of Gannon Theological Seminary for 18 years. A dignified, well-educated man, he was her mentor as a young woman. Dr. Jones' wife was a local schoolteacher. When his wife had to rise early for her teaching schedule, Dr. Jones would often ask Cynthia to accompany him to community events held in the evening. Her exposure to civic, educational and business interests gave Cynthia a broader view of the world. *"My uncle was very well-respected in the community. People would always take my call when I used his name as a reference. Having access to key contacts certainly helped me in my young career. I hope to leave that legacy of respect to my nieces and nephews."*

Cynthia credits her family's love, support, and strong spiritual foundation with much of who she is. *"I used to be a worrier. But as I have grown in my faith I have come to understand that to worry is a show of your lack of faith. No matter what happens, I know that God will take care of us according to His will."* Being a positive and uplifting person is important to her in her relationships with others. She believes that attitude is life's framework.

## ▶ CYNTHIA THE INDIVIDUAL

Today, you might see Cynthia driving around town in her new Jaguar, which she fully enjoys but does not hold in the highest esteem. *"I drive it like a truck! Sure, I enjoy it, but it is just a thing after all."* Her perspective on the trappings of success is in line with her spiritual and philosophical approach to life. *"God has blessed me to allow me to succeed, but it's the people in your life that really matter."* She adds that people need to remember their softer, gentler side . . . that they are individuals with emotions and desires; they are not their job.

High energy, trim, beautiful, wise, focused, deliberate, clear, directed . . . these are the words her friends and coworkers would use to describe this dynamic individual. Her focused and independent style has been her ally in business, although she wonders as a single woman if men realize how multi-dimensional women really are. *"I hope to be united one day with a life mate, but it would be inappropriate not to glorify the talent God has given me by minimizing my accomplishments to win the favor of a man."* She explains that she is patient and will wait for the man God is preparing for her.

Cynthia's business side is complimented by her feminine approach to her private life where she enjoys travel, reading, spending time with her family, painting and indulging her love of entertaining. A party at her house would include a mixed group of friends or family who would be treated to dining with fine china, cloth napkins, name plates set for guests, musical accompaniment, and Cynthia's famous salmon, grits, quiche and fine cuisine.

Reflecting on her life, Cynthia feels happy and blessed with her abilities, achievements, friends and family. Wise beyond her years, some have told her she has "an old soul".

Looking ahead, she is having her home studio expanded to allow her more room for painting. She has always enjoyed fine art and has several pieces of her own work hanging on the walls of her home. *"I don't mind working. I have always worked hard, but in the future I hope to enjoy more balance and free time as I get closer to my retirement years."*

## ▶ SUCCESS SECRETS FOR OTHER WOMEN

- *"We may not all want to be entrepreneurs, but we all have the ability to support a business and be a catalyst in the place we work. When women foster undercurrents against other women and let the green-eyed monster get in the way, they hold back women everywhere"*
- *"It's all about attitude and performance. Sow the seeds of success to be the best you can be in whatever life choices you make."*
- *"Don't take life too seriously and don't make everything personal.*
- *Make a decision. If it is a good one, build on it. If it is a bad one, grow from it.*
- *"Spend time with other professionals and high achievers. Sharing their challenges will give your life perspective."*
- *"Monitor your finances. If you don't have it, don't spend it. Don't mix your personal accounts with the business accounts."*
- *"Be consistent. Work hard. Enjoy life now!"*
- *"Remember that passion is about more than just feeling strongly about your career. If your goals and dreams are important to you, be willing to suffer for them. Your commitment to your dreams will turn suffering into joy."*

By her own account, she has worked diligently through 11 years with her partner to build equity and credibility for their business through top-level performance. With the foundation years completed, she sees the next challenge is to maintain and grow the capabilities of the firm and the people who work with her there. Cynthia shares that she prays every day to make the best decisions for her team and to be the best employer that she can be. If all goes well in Cynthia Jones' plans, God will hear the words of this strong, black woman in Atlanta, Georgia and continue to show her the way.

> *"Identify your motive. If it will make a better world, love it completely. Nourish it."*

**Victoria MacKenzie-Childs**

# MacKenzie-Childs

Starving artist was not just a figure of speech in Victoria MacKenzie-Childs' young adult life. The narrative of her emergence into the business world is a poignant tale of artistic dedication, sensitivity, talent and determination to succeed inspired by her love for her daughter, Heather.

The story of Victoria MacKenzie-Childs is set in her own

childhood. Born in San Francisco and reared in Los Altos, her earliest memories are of life growing up in what is now known as Silicon Valley, when it was a rural area with rolling apricot orchards. Her family lived in comfortable, refined surroundings. Life was civilized and enjoyable. Art, music, dance and spirituality were mainstays in the family routines evidenced by family pastimes experimenting with artistic materials, singing and time spent in spiritual reflection.

The family always dressed for Sunday dinner and the children were expected to report on an article they had read before the meal would begin. In the same screen, Victoria's mother had been a childhood performer, dancing with the Taylor Sisters at soldier's bases and singing in radio performances. In all, life was principled but joyful.

When she was 13 years old, the MacKenzie family relocated to Madison, Indiana for Victoria's father's career as he accepted a position with a friend who was opening a manufacturing business there. Life changed dramatically. While the family values remained the same, their world turned into a more humble, idyllic Huck Finn story with long lazy Midwest summer days on the Ohio river and winters devoted to 4-H activities like cooking, sewing and tending to farm animals. Victoria loved this new routine and the spontaneous fun it brought into her childhood experience. Hers was the best of all worlds as she remembers it and reminisces on her mother's photograph taken wearing a silk suit and high heels with Victoria's brother's 4-H prize steer. *"We laughed whether we thought of ourselves as city sophisticates or country folk."*

During early elementary school, Victoria was not much interested in academics. She was demurring and unsure of herself.

In the seventh grade, a teacher opened a door to her growth by asking Victoria if she would give the prayer for the Thanksgiving assembly. When she addressed the school with the hymn she had memorized, it was a turning point in her confidence and purpose. After years of poor grades, she ended up graduating at the top of her class. To this day, she is grateful for her parents' patience and support nurturing her creativity and growth through those early years.

Victoria went on to Indiana University for her undergraduate studies in theater and fine arts, and later, attended Radcliff College in Boston to begin her graduate work in art. At the time she had also secured a part-time teaching position at the Massachusetts College of Art. It was here that she met Richard Childs, who was a student there. Ironically, Victoria shared studio space with Richard and attempted to match him up with her roommate, Margaret, when they first met. Richard had other ideas and proposed to Victoria within the first months of their relationship. They were married within a month and one-half. Their mutual passion for work in sculpture and art and their love for one another grew from those early days working side by side in the studio together.

After they were married, the couple decided to continue their graduate work at Alfred University in western New York, which was renowned for its studies in ceramic science and art. At that time, ceramics and sculpture were still not regarded as authentic "art" because they used craft material, clay, as their medium. This was thought of as a means to functional, reproductive outputs only. Nevertheless, the MacKenzie-Childs transferred to Alfred University to pursue their specialization.

Victoria's study there involved work with heavy, dirty

mounds of clay. She was the first married woman in her graduate program. The other male students did not interact with her
in their predominantly "boys club" atmosphere. For the most
part, she worked quietly and seriously alone. (She had no desire
to be outspoken or rebellious about her position as class outcast
in this scenario.) By then, Victoria and Richard had a newborn
child, Heather, who was their focus in any free time away from
their study and work.

To help support one another while they studied at Alfred,
Victoria made porcelain boxes and sold them in a shop on Madison Avenue in New York. Richard was a short-order cook to help
support them during these graduate school years. While the sale
of decorative boxes helped the couple survive, it was not considered acceptable to sell craft to make a living at that time. The
only accepted career pursuit in the serious art world was the
role of teacher and artist with the end product created only for
the satisfaction of the galleries.

## ▶ AN ABUNDANCE OF TEACHERS

When both Richard and Victoria had completed graduate school
and their masters' degrees in fine arts, they looked for one of the
coveted teaching positions that would allow them to carry on
with the work they were passionate about. Unfortunately, they
came to a dead end rather quickly. There were no jobs to be had
in the United States. Using money they had received as graduation gifts, the couple and their child moved to Europe to visit
friends and explore career opportunities there. Their last resort
was work in a commercial production pottery in Devon, Eng-

land. They were also hired on to teach ceramics at the Torquay Technical College.

A strange chapter in her life, Victoria suggests that she regarded it as a cultural experience working with the local people and observing them in their native setting. While in England, Victoria also designed clothes and sent them off to be sold in New York for added income. After two years, the pottery closed and the young family returned to the U.S. looking for work.

In 1980, a teaching position became available at Wells College in Aurora, New York, a small town located in the Finger Lakes region. Richard applied for it and was hired on for a salary as a part-time professor making $4,000 per year. It wasn't much, but it was all they had. Their artists' discipline echoed the sentiment that *if you love your work you shouldn't care about the money.* This life was *definitely not* all about the money. They continued on for love of their artists' work.

The MacKenzie-Childs found an old 19th century neglected farmhouse in the middle of a cornfield that had not been lived in for 40 years. This became their home. It was humble. Their source of heat was a wood-burning stove that burned when the family could afford wood. Furnishings consisted only of second hand odds and ends they collected that no one else wanted. Fresh paint on the walls in bright colors and art accents here and there would serve as adornments to the simple dwelling.

## ▶ THE STARVING ARTISTS YEARS

Richard taught and sculpted. Victoria continued designing clothes and selling them for extra money. Late at night and in her spare time she would work on her own ceramics and sculpture portfolio. Heather, their daughter, worked around the home with her mother. The family did not have a television set, as a reflection of their personal philosophy, "to keep home a haven, free of the onslaught of materialism and worldliness." Heather's life was simple, but happy. She was totally engaged in whatever activity in which she participated whether at work or at play.

Life was very difficult for Victoria in that old farmhouse. She worked hard at being a supportive wife, a good mother, a seamstress and an artist with very little resources to support her. She remembers crying when she had to work with fine silk fabrics after her hands had become scratched and rough from molding clay for her sculpture. At one point, she had reached the end of her patience with this life of constant rushing between work commitments and took notice of her young daughter at play. *"I noticed how she was totally present in whatever activity she participated in. Whether working or playing, she just enjoyed the moment for what it was and didn't worry about the next part of the daily routine."* Heather's example gave Victoria new energy and resilience as she tried to reach more harmony with her work and self-expression.

Heather asked for very little as a child. She was raised to interpret Christmas as a time of giving. You can imagine in this dire financial situation, she had few toys. Her early childhood days were filled with helping her parents and her simple life around the farmhouse. In her elementary school years, Heather managed to arrange her class schedule to attend the local school in the morning and take classes at the local college in French, German, piano, recorder and ballet in the afternoon. It was unconventional, but it worked.

When she was eight years old, her aunt sent her a book

about the Royal Ballet School in London. This book became a focal point in Heather's life. She carried the book with her everywhere and dreamed of studying at the Royal Ballet. She practiced her ballet positions using the footboard of her bed as her barre. Eventually, she asked her mother if she truly could go to London to study dance. Victoria knew that Heather had never asked for much for herself. She wanted to help with this childhood dream, but replied that she *"would have to find the way there on your own."*

And she did. The next summer Heather uncovered overgrown wild raspberry bushes on the farm property. Each day, she picked the fruit and brought it into the village in her little red wagon. She even made up business cards and distributed them so that orders could be telephoned in to her. She was dedicated and determined to earn the money she needed for ballet school. The raspberry bushes thrived like they never had before or have since, responding to the love and care of this little girl with a dream and a need for their growth.

At the end of the summer, Heather had earned $350 in cash, a sum of money the family had not seen in quite a long time. It may not seem like much now, but then, it was enough to pay for her airfare, tuition and a second-hand uniform for the ballet school of her dreams. It was enough but there were no extra dollars for parents' airfares.

## ▶ *A PAINFUL DEPARTURE*

There was no turning back on a promise to the child. Off she went to London on her own as a ten-year old child. When Victoria and Richard tearfully saw her off at the airport, they realized they had no money to plan their next visit with their little girl. In their grief at her departure, Richard spoke up and said, "If we have to make teacups to see her again, we will!" Victoria only hoped that he meant it.

In her mindset, Victoria was somewhat torn between wanting to go forward as an individual with a creative, new idea in a successful art and business venture and, at the same time, wanting to stay in sync with her relationship with her husband. She was also reluctant to veer out of the traditional art world alone.

One day, Richard did come home with a teacup he had made and placed it on the kitchen table in their home. Victoria was elated but silent. She waited. Weeks passed. Nothing happened. This was not the start of a business, but rather a singular piece of art. She prayed. She cried. It was a long, cold winter missing Heather and living their meager subsistence.

On another occasion, when she was at a low point emotionally living in their cold home, Victoria could stand by patiently no longer. Her clay had frozen because there was no heat. She missed Heather terribly. She reached out and made a phone call on their four-party line to a Christian Science practitioner who was a family friend. As she sobbed and shared her desperate story, he encouraged her to be grateful for the quiet time to pray, reflect and prepare for the weeks ahead. He expressed that if she were quiet and introspective now, it would give her strength for the busy time that was in store for her. His words turned out to be prophetic.

Three months later, Victoria was in her studio working and listening to classical music on an old radio. At the introduction of the performance the announcer explained that "today's opera is La Boheme, the story of how the artist is never accepted by society and eventually the artist starves and dies." It was as if a light went on in Victoria's mind. This was the start or the end of something as she knew it.

*"A spirit rose up within me as I turned off the radio and declared that I will never listen to that type of thinking again. Art can serve society and we are artists that will not die as we bring our work into other's lives."* Victoria was determined. She would survive and thrive as an artist, even if it meant going against the binding traditional roles of old art circles. Best of all, she knew then she would earn enough money to see her daughter again soon.

She immediately began making a terra cotta bowl. *"I was energized by my passion and the work was great fun. The room filled with sunshine and the whole studio was dancing."* This first bowl, an oval "chowder bowl", was the start of the Victoria MacKenzie-Childs signature pottery collection and is still a mainstay today.

## ▶ SHAPES OF THINGS TO COME

Victoria found new energy in her passion for self-expression in her work that had become as enjoyable as time spent at play. She hoped that Richard would approve of her new direction. While he did not disapprove, he was not as enthusiastic for her work as she was. She continued at full speed in any case, and shared some of her designs with a friend. He cautioned her not to let galleries and the art world see what she was doing because it was functional pottery. (In the art world, Victoria had broken all the rules by following this path of self-expression.) Blinded by her love of the work and passionate about finding a means to bring in needed dollars for airfare to see Heather, Victoria went on and developed a complete line of signature ceramics that reflected the beauty and joy she found everywhere in her new world view. *"How can something so good do harm?"* This was the question she kept asking herself as she continued to develop new pieces in the line.

When she had accumulated a range of designs in her ceramic pottery line of dinnerware and gift items, Victoria returned to the shop on Madison Avenue in New York, The Gazebo, where she had sold ceramic boxes to help support Richard when he was in graduate school. The shop was supported by wealthy philanthropists, Gloria Vanderbilt and Lynn Barnard, who created it as an outlet for women in Appalachia to sell their wares to upscale New York City customers.

As Victoria unpacked her pieces to show the shop owners, she set them out in a corner of the room. Customers streamed in to see what the new items were. Soon, a crowd gathered. Everyone was intrigued and excited by the new, unconventional and attractive original designs of Victoria MacKenzie-Childs. Before she had left, over $7,000 in goods was sold to the customers who flocked in the door that day. A new business was born and there was no turning back for Victoria. Her first thought was, *"We can see Heather now."*

## ▶ PRODUCTION AND PROMOTION

The next challenge would clearly be to create enough pieces to meet the demand the first order and subsequent ones would require. Victoria realized she could not do it all alone. She immediately hired two student helpers who she planned to have help her paint her signature designs on pieces fired in a nearby pottery. Unfortunately, the pottery could not accommodate her needs and it was necessary that she find a means to fire the shapes using their own kiln and resources. Richard pitched in and helped make the basic pots and forms needed after hours at school. This would only serve as a temporary solution.

Soon Victoria's work required that they set up a pottery in the village of Aurora. Early quarters were set up in the cellar of the Fargo Bar, space they could use as long as they paid to keep the furnace running in the old facility. Victoria recalls beer bottle caps dropping through the floorboards of the bar, down from the basement rafters and onto their work area. It was a good start. Dedicated workers kept pieces in production from early morning until well into the night.

After the first year in the cellar of the Fargo Bar, the business moved into four floors of an old Wells College dormitory that was rented for $500 per month. Demand continued. The business grew. Victoria's brother took samples with him to gift shops along the route of a cross-country vacation trip he had planned. Victoria was still leading the effort, but soon, Richard took a year off from his teaching to help her. He still hadn't fully committed to the new work, but he could see that his support was needed and offered to help out.

It was a lonely time. When Richard did not wholeheartedly embrace her new venture early on, it was difficult for Victoria. She did not want to go on alone. When she was tired and lonely she told herself that she did not want to keep providing for the family. But her spirit and a voice inside her urged her on. *"Eventually I realized that I could take the lead and carry on alone if I had to. It was a great comfort to me when Richard did come into the business full time and become fully a part of it."* Victoria reflects that Richard's support and his technical expertise with production, as well as his own creative and inventive spirit, have been of great value as the business has grown.

## ▶ TRADE SHOW TURNING POINT

In 1984, someone mentioned to Victoria that she should bring the works to a trade show, The New York Gift Show, one of the most prestigious of its kind in the nation. Her first thought was to forget the idea since it was such a commercial commitment. (She was still working on sculptural pieces in the evening. She thought of the pottery as a sideline, a vehicle for a reunion with Heather.) *Accent On Design* was the theme of the show. Working through her reluctance, she decided to go.

They did not have any existing display structures for the line, so Richard and Victoria built a home set that was quite elaborate to showcase the work. Once built, they transported the pieces of it on their Chevette and traveled to the show looking like a circus wagon. This trade show set was so dramatic that it brought immediate attention at the show and launched the pottery in dramatic style.

The booth was filled with people throughout the show. Victoria was overwhelmed by the response, particularly since she was not used to being with the public all day. While wedged in the corner by the thrust of the crowd, she was approached by the divisional merchandise manager for Nieman Marcus, an upscale department store that was then predominantly in operation out west. He had dashed in to see what all the commotion was about and was amazed at the fresh, beautiful new work. When he handed his card to Victoria she just set it aside. She had never heard of Nieman Marcus and had no experience in following up on such leads.

Realizing that she was not aware of the importance of the meeting, the Nieman Marcus representative decided to pursue Victoria. Her fresh work would bring an edge to the store's upscale gift gallery. At his insistence, Cynthia Marcus, who was responsible for the gift department, contacted Victoria and Richard and arranged to purchase the work. This was a turning point for the MacKenzie-Childs Ltd. collection as it became available for sale in one of the country's leading department stores. Within weeks the first large order came in. From that time on, the growth of their business was unstoppable.

## ▶ A GRADUAL EVOLUTION

Since the early building years, much has changed for the growing company. Richard joined the business full-time much to Victoria's delight and his artistic experience and management support have been valuable to her. They both learned the business as time went on. Working side by side again just as in their first art studio, they have continued on as a team leading their new venture together. As needed, artistic, production and management staff were added.

In 1985, it was necessary to find larger quarters to expand the design, production and distribution facilities. While driving through the Aurora countryside they came upon a rolling 85-acre dairy farm property with a number of large barns that could be renovated to meet their needs. The site on Lake Cayuga became a perfect setting for the creative process which eventually would feature extensive gardens and lakes, now stocked with ducks, geese, turkeys and an array of exotic animals including peacocks, Toulouse geese and Highland cattle.

This creative setting was the breeding ground for product line expansion and freedom of thought for Victoria and Richard's design work. Today, the MacKenzie-Childs Ltd. collection includes a colorful array of ceramic and pottery dinnerware in hand-painted majolica design, as well as candlesticks, lamps, glass, ornaments, furniture, linens and gifts.

The bright colors and mix of unusual shapes and lines reflect the thinking of Victoria who is committed to maintaining a childlike love of art, supported by Richard's genius for creative execution. Together, they blend to find beauty in an array of designs in unconventional, whimsical style. Checks, dots and swirls often live side by side on the unusual pieces bearing their name. A glass-topped table with a porcelain base, a wooden chair with a fish shape for its back support area, fish-shaped sink basins are all designs that challenge the need for art to be conventional. Their work brings the freedom of the gypsies and the mixed hues of a field of wildflowers into expression in signature collections.

In 1993, the line had gained such popular acceptance that the collection was sold in its own store in a posh Madison Avenue, New York shop. Subsequently another MacKenzie-Childs shop was opened on Rodeo Drive in California.

Today, the company employs about 300 employees at its 100,000 square foot headquarters and retail locations. While there have been highs and lows along the way the challenges were taken on and the victories celebrated with their staff. (In 1993, a devastating fire burned the Aurora studio to the ground. Everyone pitched in and the building was eventually rebuilt.)

## ❭ *REFLECTIONS OF THE ARTIST*

Victoria is a soft-spoken personification of the colorful art she has crafted inspired by her daughter. Bright hair highlighted in an array of colors, checked tights and whimsical attire are the accoutrements one comes to expect upon meeting her. An eye for design and appreciation for the natural beauty in the world are apparent in her extensive work. As her collection has grown, so too has the artist. She has these words of advice to share with other women who are considering starting a business of their own.

- *"Don't let your own thinking hold you back as a limitation on what you can do with your life."*
- *"Challenge builds strength."*
- *"We measured success early on by reaching our goals."*
- *"Live in the present and give of yourself to get the most out of life."*
- *"Keep an eye on your spending as your company grows."*
- *"Trust the spiritual truth and a strong foundation will be there for support."*

A final word about Heather, the beautiful child who inspired this success story: Victoria and Richard did visit her in Europe one year after they sent her off alone to study ballet. She continued to study abroad for several years subsequently and later, married a young man from France of Swedish and French descent. Now 28 years old, Heather and Nils have a daughter of their own. The couple lives a transatlantic lifestyle spending half of their time in Paris and half in New York. On a happy note, the young family is expecting the birth of another child soon.

# ▶ *ENDINGS AND BEGINNINGS*

Throughout the story of the founding and growth of MacKenzie-Childs, Ltd., there have been ups and downs as in any business, as in life. In 2001, after sustaining a serious financial loss in two commercial real estate transactions, MacKenzie-Childs was in financial straits and was moved into receivership by their bank. To the dismay of the company founders, the financial institution exercised its right to sell the company prior to the final hearing requested by Victoria and Richard during which they had hoped to buy back the company they had created. On June 3, 2001, MacKenzie-Childs Ltd. was sold. The company's founders are no longer officially associated with the organization that bears their name.

While it was with great sadness that they met and ultimately accepted this occurrence, Victoria and Richard are already in planning for a new artistic endeavor that will align itself with a non-profit charity for children. They believe that their artistic spirit and dedication, along with their extensive network of friends, supporters, distributors and business associates will be the foundation for an exciting new artistic initiative. While the details of this venture are still unfolding, the spirit, creativity, dedication and positive energy of this dynamic artistic team will continue on as it takes new shape in the months and years to come.

> *"Success is found in a good balance between your business and family life."*

**Rian van Velzen-Bastiaansen**

# Nature's Choice

Sometimes a great idea presents itself by surprise. This was the case for Rian van Velzen-Bastiaansen of the Netherlands, when she and her future husband took a holiday vacation to hike and relax in Switzerland in 1994. Rian was working as an export manager for a Japanese noodle company in Holland. Her fiancé, Mark, was a marketing executive in a major telecommunications firm. Both had demanding careers and were looking forward to the time to take a break from their regular routines.

When they checked into the family run chalet that was to be their lodging they found the owners to be most accommodating. What was particularly delightful was the heated pillow that was brought to their room each evening to warm the cold Swiss nights. The chalet kitchen was heated by an enormous oven, called a "kaminen-kachel", that was used for cooking and for heating the kitchen area. A compartment in the rear of the oven was large enough to gently heat the special pillows that were stuffed with dried cherry pits, a substance that offered a pleasant aroma and a continued heat source once warmed. Rian and Mark inquired and learned that the pillows were hand made by the grandmother of the chalet owner.

The warm cherry pit pillow was such a pleasant experience that they asked if they could buy several to give to their own grandparents as Christmas gifts. Unfortunately, the chalet owners were not interested in selling any of their pillows.

Upon their return to Holland, the couple decided they would try to make such a pillow themselves since they had never seen or experienced anything like it prior to their trip. They still thought it would make a great family gift. They began experimenting with the process of drying the cherry pits, trying the oven, the microwave and slow drying outdoors in the sun. To their surprise, this was no easy task. It was difficult to dry the pits sufficiently to prevent molding. Their last resort was to ask a friend who had access to a coffee bean roaster if he would serve as their vendor to dry roast the pits. He agreed and the process was the perfect solution.

Mark's mother helped with the experiment and sewed a pillow form out of basic cotton cloth. In short order, there were ten cherry pit pillows completed for holiday gifts. All of the individuals who received the special pillows were extremely pleased to receive them. In fact, they were such a big hit, Rian decided to pull together materials for another order and attempt to sell them at a local consumer trade show. She remarked casually that if there was a great demand for them, she might just quit her job and start a business manufacturing and selling the cherry pit pillows. Little did she know that her remark was prophetic of things to come.

In the early months of manufacturing, pillows could be made fairly inexpensively. Cherry pits were available at no charge then from food manufacturers. (Later, after the first year, these suppliers would come to charge for treated and cleaned cherry pits.) Cotton cloth could be bought at wholesale prices. Labor was secured from a handicapped community center in Holland that was looking for such work for their organization. In short, it was not difficult to pull together a large quantity of pillows for the trade show.

The product, which she called "Hittepit", was an immediate success. It was unique in the insulating properties of the all-natural cherry pits. Its ability to conform to the body was a feature that was well received for its comfort and massage applications. Rian's and Mark's mothers worked the show floor during the daytime; the young couple took over the booth for the evening shifts. Over 25 pillows were sold each day for five days at 25 guilders each, a profitable venture for the new little company. After the show, people were inquiring at local stores as to how to obtain such a pillow. Demand rose quickly and Rian realized that it was time she made good on her promise to devote herself full-time to the cherry pit pillow business. Nature's Choice became a full-time operation.

Her family thought she was crazy. Her fiancée gave her his full support and could see the potential this product had for a new business. On January 1, 1995, Rian took the step to become an entrepreneur and didn't look back. She figured that if this venture did not prove to be successful, she could always find another position in traditional business. Success would be a constant in the years that followed.

By the end of the first year, pillow sales had grossed 100,000 guilders. (Guilders were trading at about $2.50 for an American dollar at the time of this interview.) By early 1996, products and shipping boxes had taken over Rian's living room to the extent that she decided to find commercial space at a location that was five minutes from home. For the next several years, pillow sales continued to flourish. The product was sold at trade fairs all over Holland. A "part-time" staff person was added who would immediately be needed and moved to "full-time" status as she helped in every aspect of the business. New pillow shapes and sizes including squares, oblongs, valentines, U-shapes and hand warmers were added to the line in that timeframe. Along the way, Rian and Mark were married. After a brief honeymoon, the work at hand continued on.

As the business grew, so too did its product line. A soothing eye pillow was added next, the Snoozie pillow filled with flaxseed slipped into a cover material of 100% silk. Its unique combination of weight and design offered a soothing and cooling effect for tired eyes. Soon, the Bucky Pillow was brought into the line, a specially designed pillow filled with 100% natural buckwheat hulls for support that conforms to the shape of the body. Rian and Mark collaborated on the planning of each new product. All new additions were evaluated on their match with the company's core mission, which was to "Provide Healthware and Bodycare Products to Make Daily Life More Pleasant."

In 1998, the company reached one million guilders in annual sales. The following year, Mark joined the business full-time to help run the growing organization. Today, the company's revenues are in the range of seven million guilders. Nature's Choice employs 14 people on staff full-time and uses the original community center and commercial seamstresses to produce their products.

Over the years, Bath Tea, Bubbling Bath Balls, and Eye Tea were added to the mix of offerings to bring relaxation and pleasure to the customer. Special items were also brought in to help with cold winters and hot summers. Hotsocks, a product that can be microwaved, were brought on as the body care solution to cold or aching feet. Neck and Wrist Coolers were added to the Nature's Choice group to bring immediate cooling to users who wear them on their neck or wrist to cool down after sports or in hot, humid weather. These are a sampling of the company's portfolio of products. New items are always being added.

Today, the company's products are sold directly only in the business-to-business arena, although they may be found in stores like the Body Shop, Sephora, health stores and pharmacies throughout Europe in countries including Holland, Germany, Belgium, France, Sweden and the United Kingdom. While they are not sold to distributors in the United States yet, it is likely Nature's Choice may enter that market in the years ahead. *"Opportunity is everywhere,"* Rian remarks, *"so we attempt to be thoughtful about the growth and scope of our business."* The company is currently in the process of strategic planning to define the optimal growth rate and positioning for the line in years to come.

### ▶ PERSONAL THOUGHTS

As Rian's career saw significant changes over the years, so too did her personal life. Rian and Mark now have three children, Max, Kasper, and Tess. Childcare is an issue the couple must plan for. At this time, a babysitter comes to their home three days each week to help with the children. One day a week the little ones are taken to a day care center. Rian is currently working in the office four days per week.

When asked her opinion as to whether being a woman in business was an obstacle, she replied that she would like more time with her children, but is committed to the success of the business as well. It's a balance issue she works hard to keep in line.

From a business standpoint, gender has not been a primary issue for Rian. *"It's all about your spirit and enthusiasm for what you do,"* she reflects. *"There were obstacles that we had to handle early on, but they were not gender based. If you have a good idea and persevere, nothing can stop your success but your own mindset."*

In addition to perseverance, her personal key to success has been in responding to people, including the customer and the company staff. She sees any business as a living thing that is always growing and changing over time. In that environment, teamwork has been tied into the company's values and approach. A young team, Mark is the oldest on board at age 37, and the company associates work hard, are enthusiastic, and enjoy one another.

In spite of the great time demands of running a business and being the mother of small children, Rian tries to find time to entertain friends in her free time as a break from her responsibilities.

## ▶ THOUGHTS FOR SHARING

Rian encourages other women entrepreneurs to turn to their local chamber of commerce and to professional networking associations in the early years particularly of running a new business. Her experience with the Innovation Center at her local chamber offered her valuable guidance when she was just starting out. Likewise, the colleagues she gained through the UVON international businesswomen's organization have been quite valuable in her personal and professional development.

Other thoughts she would like to share follow here.

- *"Success is satisfaction with what you are doing with your life. For me, a good balance between my family and business life is my personal success."*
- *"Time solves all problems."*
- *"Respond to your customers but keep in touch with who you are and what your core business really is."*
- *"Learn about all aspects of your business to manage it effectively."*
- *"Be prepared for your business to go through growth stages along the way."*
- *"My passion in life is my family."*
- *"You will never know the extent of your possible success unless you follow your dreams."*
- *"Ultimately the responsibility for your company's success will always be yours."*
- *"Just do it."*

At the end of the day, when Rian van Velzen-Bastiaansen finally puts her head on a pillow to get her likely much needed sleep, one can only wonder if she will dream up yet another creative new product to improve the quality of life of her customers for their improved health and well being. If her pillow is cherry pit or buckwheat filled it may be the backdrop for yet another great new idea that will present itself, like its predecessors, by surprise. What won't be a surprise is that Rian's life will continue to unfold in an interesting fashion. Sweet dreams are her product's destination after all.

*"My career has become a life work, not a job".*

**Barbara Mowat**

# Home Business Report

Barbara Mowat spent fifteen years teaching and counseling students and adults in Vancouver, Canada schools and colleges before taking her own counsel and following her dream of starting a business of her own. Early on, she had decided to be a school counselor and teacher as a means to help raise her three children while working in a career that would be "family friendly". A psychology major by training, Barbara eventually found herself at Douglas College counseling others about their careers, while realizing that her own life passion was to be an entrepreneur.

Responsible, caring, committed, and intense are the qualities that come to mind when you get to know this focused individual. When Barbara made up her mind to enter the business world, there was no doubt she was prepared to work hard until she reached success. Having encouraged others to build on their personal strengths, expertise and experience, she chose a logical bridge for herself, took a leave of absence from her senior faculty position, and began a human resources and training company that she could launch from home.

Barbara's home address was a key motivator for her decision to start a company. As a young woman, she had moved from Ontario, where she was raised, to the province of British Columbia and the small town of Abbottsford, which is located 70 miles east of Vancouver. Abbottsford was not a major metropolitan area and consequently, it did not offer the career opportunities for teaching or business that Vancouver held for the region. For 15 years, Barbara had to deal with a 140-mile round trip commute over highways and bridges to work and back, even in the harsh winter weather of the Pacific Northwest. By the time she decided to make the move to business, she had grown tired of the driving and was inspired to find a creative solution.

Given that home-based businesses back in 1996 had a negative connotation, Barbara knew that she would need a Vancouver address to gain the respect of her target business market, so she secured a post office box to create a "virtual city office". At the same time, she continued to set up her actual day-to-day operation at home.

Impact Communications opened for business in 1987 fully equipped with a firm resolve, a new personality assessment product that Barbara had helped to develop with several colleagues at the university, and a portfolio of skills to offer businesses. While the phone was ringing and work was being generated, within three months, Barbara realized that with the $5000 she borrowed to start the business, she did not have the capital base to sustain startup. Fortunately, Douglas College called her at that time to see if she would be interested in running a community continuing education program they were planning to offer. Barbara agreed, under the terms that she could continue to run her own fledgling business at the same time, a rigorous schedule that she kept for 13 months.

After the first full year running Impact Communications, Barbara determined that she needed to diversify her services. At the same time, she observed from her work at the college that many small single industry towns in northwest Canada were struggling economically. Large employers in forestry and mining were closing their doors. Community residents needed to develop new business opportunities of their own if they wanted to remain living in the area.

A trip to the Safeway grocery store was the moment that brought Barbara's thinking to a new level. She purchased a *Ladies Home Journal* magazine that featured home-based business growth in the United States. It was clear to her at that time that Canada was not as serious or advanced in this business approach as was the U.S. and that there was an opportunity for Barbara to help develop this source of revenue for the Canadian economy. After reading the article, she called Barbara Brabeck from Naperville (IL) and Joanne Pratt from Dallas (TX), the women featured in the article, and began research on how to create these types of opportunities. The question she asked was *"Who else is doing something from home and how can we make this work more effectively in Canada?"*

Coincidentally, shortly after this "supermarket moment", the Ministry of Regional Economic Development called the college where Barbara was working and asked whether they had a resource person who could help them develop the home-based business opportunities particularly needed in remote, small Canadian towns. The college referred them to Barbara who was in the midst of her research on the subject. She recommended that the government initiate a complete background study, and develop a plan and a set of tools including seminars and publications to help home-based business to establish roots, to create a market and to prosper in Canada. In 1987, to fully answer the ministry's question, Barbara put together a national study of what was needed including changes in legislation that would enable an economic model to empower home based businesses. By 1990, over 90% of the initiatives she recommended came to fruition, largely through the work of Impact Communications. The array of tools, training and approaches that were developed within this effort positioned Barbara and her team as the world's leader in providing programs and services for home-based businesses to thrive and bring their products to market.

## ▶ *TRADE SHOWS MAKE THE DIFFERENCE*

Of all the tools created by Impact Communications in this work, perhaps the most powerful one was their development of wholesale trade shows to open sales distribution channels to home based entrepreneurs. In 1989, the team launched the first "Uniquely B.C. Show", featuring the products and crafts of home-based businesses in British Columbia. The show was such a great success that the local Alberta economic development officials asked Impact Communications to create "Uniquely Alberta". Others followed in rapid succession including "Uniquely Prairies" and "Uniquely Ontario". Word spread internationally, and "Uniquely Asia", "Uniquely Puerto Rico" and "Uniquely Slovenia" followed lead by Impact Communications expertise.

The service provided for home-based businesses in this trade show format revolved around the development of their approach in preparation for a business-to-business show debut. At the same time, Impact Communications helped micro business owners tie in to a strong wholesale distribution chain. Prior to participating in a "Uniquely" show, first-time entrepreneur exhibitors receive extensive training using materials created by Barbara and her team for business planning, product development and marketing.

After customized counsel prior to the event, products are sent in advance for review by the "Uniquely" team. The fee for this training and trade show space rental for first-time participants was at the time of this interview, an unbelievably low cost of about $150, an amount only made possible by the show underwriters, major corporations that subsidize the "Uniquely" program in exchange for high visibility with growing new businesses in that given region. After the first show, this fee reverts back to a more traditional show reservation fee.

Uniquely Show corporate sponsors have included a respected lineup of companies including Royal Bank of Canada, Bank of Montreal, IBM, TELUS and AOL Canada, to name a few. In addition to providing needed funding for Uniquely program sponsorship, these business supporters play a key role in ultimately sustaining economic development for the regions they serve.

### ▶ HOME BUSINESS REPORT TAKES OFF

This goal of "sustainable economic development" is the vision that keeps pulling Barbara Mowat further into the world of micro business. Her passion and commitment to help individuals and communities nurture business startups have been evidenced in all of her work under the banner of Impact Communications. One of her most well known strategies to advance her goals has been her development of the *Home Business Report;* a quarterly publication began in 1989, when home-based business was just a "blip" on the screen of public consciousness. Originally written for British Columbia, Canada, it began as *The B.C. Home Business Report* but grew to serve a larger national audience. Within five years it grew in popularity and demand throughout the country. Today it has achieved a circulation of 50,000 readers.

*Home Business Report* is a classic home-based business in its own right. It originated out of Barbara Mowat's Impact Communications home office. Support staff also work from their homes in locations across the country. The Managing Editor works from her home in Victoria, British Columbia, where she links with writers from all over Canada and assembles an editorial plan each year. The Executive Editor works out of a home office in Toronto, Ontario. Delta, British Columbia is the location of the home office of the publication's Art Director who collaborates with classified and display advertising Sales Executives who also work from their home offices. A commercial printer, not a home-based business prints the publication.

Over the years, Barbara has continually developed trade shows and publications to help Canadian business. In spite of an intentionally chosen low profit margin to maximize her impact within the small business arena, after 10 years, Barbara's business reached the one million dollar mark in annual sales.

Along with her work delivering Impact Communications shows and publications, she has also addressed numerous business audiences in locations throughout the world including Switzerland, France, Slovenia, and Brunei. Lessons learned in Canada appear to have broad application to economic development in many countries. In 1993, she received the "Canadian Woman Entrepreneur of the Year Award for Impact on the Local Economy" in recognition of her publishing and consulting achievements helping home-based businesses fuel economic growth. Affectionately, she has come to be called the "Mother of Home-Based Business in Canada."

In 1998, Barbara's entrepreneurial spirit lead her down another path when she and her daughter, Paula, opened a Uniquely Canada retail gift shop in the small resort village of Sun Peaks, B.C. The store features a broad selection of hand crafted Canadian-made art and home décor items. Barbara owns a second home in the resort town. Decorated with products of Canadian craftsmen and women, the home has served well as a getaway for her family and herself.

# ▶ *THE WOMAN BEHIND THE MISSION*

Barbara's life in many ways prepared her for the challenging yet rewarding work that is central to her story. She learned to be a strong individual from childhood. Her mother died when Barbara was just 11 years old. The youngest of five children, she was soon called upon to help with the family chores involved in running a boarding house that they owned. Hard work was an integral part of her early years.

At age 17, Barbara eloped with a young man she had fallen in love with who also happened to be one of the boarders at her family's rental property. The young couple agreed that they would move out West to start a life together, as long as Barbara could still attend college as part of their plan. The newlyweds were poor but very happy together and committed to their goals. They rented a house for $75 per month.

Unfortunately, the birth control pills that Barbara was prescribed made her seriously ill. Not surprisingly, eleven months after their move to Abbottsford, British Columbia, the Mowat's first child, Brent, was born. Undaunted, Barbara applied for student loans and brought her baby to college classes with her when needed to keep moving toward her goal of a college education. They were still poor. Every night she scrubbed the two dozen cloth diapers they owned by hand to get ready for the baby's next day.

Two daughters soon followed, Paula and Brittany. So did Barbara's undergraduate degree in psychology and education (from Simon Fraser University) and later, a master's degree in counseling from University of British Columbia. A teaching career, 23 years of marriage to Barry (her ex-spouse who remains one of her closest friends) and a highly developed expertise in home-based business are some of the chapters in the book of her life.

Barbara's eldest daughter, Paula, was her first employee and helped in the business. At the age of 15, Paula started her own Student Secretarial Service business, which would later bring in sufficient income to pay for Paula's university tuition in full.

Brittany who is Barbara's youngest child worked part-time for mom in the early years. Today, she and Paula both work with their mother in the Impact Communications business.

Brent chose to follow in the path his father had chosen and earned his engineering technology degree to become an engineer/surveyor in Canada. Today, the Mowat "children" are 28, 25 and 31 years old.

## ▶ COUNSEL FROM THE COUNSELOR

After a full career as a teacher and counselor in the Canadian schools, Barbara is still teaching today, although her classroom is now the business world itself. Her expertise and wisdom about starting a business at home applies to any business and any entrepreneur, regardless of gender. Here is her counsel to others:

- *"People ask me what the "hot" new business is to own. I tell them to start or own a business that suits their individual goals and passion in life because you can make money doing anything. The question is, how do you want to spend your time?"*
- *"Building a business is dependent upon building relationships."*
- *"At the start, be prepared to do everything yourself."*
- *"My career has become a life work, not a job. That commitment is what is key to finding success in what you do."*

- *"The Secret of Success as I see it includes self knowledge, self discipline, perseverance, reliability, flexibility, enthusiasm and belief in yourself."*
- *"If you are not passionate about your work, you will eventually grow bored with it."*

Teacher, business professional, lecturer, mother, friend . . . no matter who you talk with about the many roles Barbara Mowat has filled in her life, the comments are always the same. She is known as a terrific, hard-working, inspiring woman who has made a difference in the growth of individuals and businesses across Canada and throughout the world. The final chapters of her professional story are still being written. It is sure to be a best seller as we continue to watch her life work make an impact on the lives of so many.

# Success Secrets

## CLUSTER FOUR—
## *The Finish Line*

▶ *SUCCESS SECRET #13: Mentors, Networks, Friends*

Starting a business and then keeping it going are no small tasks. As Lane Nemeth of Discovery Toys shared, "About every six months I would find myself exhausted by the new challenges that kept coming up." Each step of founding and running a business requires its own set of skills and expertise. The blind faith and drive needed to launch a business may be different from the role required when evaluating operational, technological or financial choices that present themselves further down the road.

One way to level out the responsibilities and mind-share required of a founder and chief executive officer is to ask mentors for an expert opinion of the business from time to time. This may take the shape of an occasional meeting with another well-respected business executive to discuss strategy and tactics or it may have a more formal structure that calls for a schedule of monthly meetings with one or more advisors. Whatever form it takes, having a mentor has been a success secret many Millionaire Women encourage.

Margaret Johnsson of The Johnsson Group believes strongly in professional mentors and has seen the power of this resource in her previous work with her early blue chip employers, Kraft and Beatrice Foods. Business mentors and professional peers are an important part of her resource group. Mary Carroll of Schoolbelles learned much during startup years from her accountant mentor who worked free of charge for Schoolbelles until the business was up and turning a profit. Today, this same accounting firm handles the company's business, as the early favor of mentoring was never forgotten. Lorraine Tribe of Australia's Quest Personnel urges women in business to find two or three respected advisors, whether men or women. In hindsight, she believes this would have helped her in the early years when it was difficult to think of everything as one individual.

Vera Bradley Designs' founders turned to a network of mentors to help plan their business from the start. SCORE, the Service Corps of Retired Executives in the United States, is a resource partner with the U.S. Small Business Administration (SBA) dedicated to aiding in the formation, growth, and success of small business nationwide. SCORE business counseling is free and confidential. The retired executives who volunteer with this organization are well versed in how to develop effective business plans and create strategies for business growth. Their mentoring is available free of charge to all U.S. citizens and can be accessed through a personal meeting, by telephone or online (www.score.org). In addition to individual counseling services, SCORE also offers informational guides including an index of useful web sites, *The Business Resource Index* and other reports. More than 4.5 million businessmen and women have been served since SCORE began counseling in 1964.

The U.S. Small Business Administration (SBA) also offers information geared specifically to the needs of women in business through the Office of Women's Business Ownership (OWBO) that offers online resource information (www.owbo@sba.gov) and individual counseling through a nationwide network of mentoring roundtables. OWBO has a women's business ownership representative in nearly every state and territory with the mission to help counsel, teach, encourage and inspire women entrepreneurs. Their Starting Courses Directory guides women through the critical steps necessary to make their business dreams come true. Courses include personal evaluation tools, strategic planning, research, trends, how to write a business plan, and legal and financial considerations, among others. Their portfolio is comprehensive and informative.

The Center for Women's Business Research, until recently known as The National Foundation for Women Business Owners (NFWBO), is another source for information, research, educational programs and consulting for women business owners. This organization will also provide information on international women's associations like Les Femmes Chefs d"Enterprises Mondiales (FCEM), Associazione Imprenditrici e Donne Dirigenti d'Azienda (AIDDA), Verband Deutscher Unternehmerinnen (VDU), The International Alliance and the Canadian Women's Business Network.

In Canada, another excellent resource for startup companies or home-based business is the *Home Based Business Report*, produced quarterly by Barbara Mowat, one of the Millionaire Women featured here. Launched in 1989 to serve British Columbia, since 1994 this report has served to help link home-based businesses throughout Canada with practical tips and advice on running a business. *Small Business Canada* (www.sbinfocanada.about.com) is another Canadian resource for information on over 700 sites offering information to small business.

Chambers of Commerce throughout the world are also good resource pools for mentors and information on business developments and best practices. To find out more about a chamber organization, check out their web site at www.uschamber.com for U.S. information and international links.

Although finding a mentor that knows you and your business well is preferred, online resources may be a good substitute for those who don't have the time, access or the inclination to develop a direct interpersonal relationship with a mentor or group of advisors.

Professional associations and networks of peers are another avenue for information and support as a business owner. The National Association of Women Business Owners (NAWBO) defines its vision as working to "propel women entrepreneurs into economic, social and political spheres of power worldwide." A national organization with chapters throughout the U.S., this group is a strong resource for women business owners offering information on marketing, finance, taxes, business planning, human resources, international trade, tech tips, client and vendor relations and available web resources. Their portfolio of benefits can be seen at their website (www.nawbo.org). A complete listing of women resource addresses and phone numbers is also available in the Resource chapter of this book.

Another excellent networking opportunity is available through the National Association for Female Executives (NAFE), the largest women's professional association and women business owners' organization in the country. NAFE provides resources and services through education, networking, and public advocacy to empower its members to achieve career success. Its web site is www.nafe.com.

Whether the organization is NAWBO, the National Association of Female Executives (NAFE), Executive Women International, a regional chamber of commerce, or a host of other professional associations that are available, the underlying value is the same if this resource is used to gather information and form relationships with peers who can assist a business owner throughout the many growth stages over the years. One caveat, unless the membership is actively *used*, dues for associations like these are overhead, not assets, for the entrepreneur member.

### ▶ SUCCESS SECRET #14:
### Nurture Your Spirit, Your Self

This success secret might seem like an obvious one, but it's not. Often, women entrepreneurs, and perhaps many women in general, forget to take time to renew and nurture themselves. The traditional role of nurturer and the combined responsibilities of family and work commitments often leave women little time to care for their own physical, mental and spiritual needs.

The Millionaire Women are attuned to this need for personal renewal even though, at times, it cannot be an everyday priority due to time constraints. Stephanie Moss of Solutions Group in South Africa explains, *"In the midst of your busy life, it is critical that you take care of yourself. After all, your health is the foundation of your success."*

A majority of the Millionaire Women foster continual improvement in their own intellectual growth and that of their staff as continuous improvement tends to be part of their company's core values.

In addition to physical rest and intellectual renewal, this success secret includes the need for spiritual renewal. Margaret Johnsson of The Johnsson Group advises, *"Believe in yourself and ask for help from others and from God to find strength and persistence."* Cynthia Jones of Jones Worley Design agrees and relies on prayer and spirituality to help her find inner strength and peace. In her own words: *"I have come to realize that worry is unhealthy and a lack of faith in the Lord. No matter what happens, I know that God will take care of us."*

Nurturing your spirit and your self may not be part of a daily routine for most women entrepreneurs, but it is a success secret that carries significant impact if overlooked for too long.

## ▶ *SUCCESS SECRET#15: Attitude is Everything*

*Believe in yourself. Be tenacious. Never give up. Help others to succeed through your own success.* These are the words of the Millionaire Women that believe that just about anything is possible with a good idea, the right attitude and a commitment to succeed. These words are echoed over and over again in conversations with this high achieving group.

Motivational speakers would agree that attitude is a powerful force in reaching a goal or a dream. Likewise the ability to motivate a group of people toward the attainment of a shared business goal is an asset that leaders use to leap up to the highest levels of success. Professional journals in the areas of psychology and business include abundant reports on the impact of attitude on everything we do.

Arlene Lenarz of Mary Kay Cosmetics speaks to choosing your attitude when she shares, *"We are not born winners or losers. We are all born choosers."* Gwen Willhite of Cookie Bouquet looks back at challenging situations and reflects, *"The names of the people who were difficult I have forgotten. Those individuals who helped me at each step I will never forget."* Gwen's wisdom is reflective of the frequent comments of the Millionaire Women encouraging their female contemporaries to support one another in the business world and not personalize disagreements or obstacles that arise. They urge other women in business to keep a sense of humor and large measure of forgiveness at hand to help refocus attitudes into a positive or constructive light.

## ▶ *SUCCESS SECRET #16: Don't Look Back*

Give your new business venture 110% of your energy and commitment and don't look back. Regrets, it appears, are not in the language of the Millionaire Women, unless they supply learning for future situations.

To give birth to a new idea and organization requires tremendous discipline, commitment and focus. Second-guessing appears to offer no charm to this group. As Rian van Velzen-Bastiaansen of Nature's Choice in Holland puts it so well, *"If your new business venture does not work out, you can always go back to your former approach to life and work for someone else. But if you keep rethinking your decision to go out on your own it will take needed energy away from your potential future success as an entrepreneur."*

Lorraine Tribe of Australia's Quest Personnel agrees, *"Don't be afraid to* start *something of your own. If you have a dream follow it and don't look back.*" Patricia Miller of Vera Bradley Designs concurs, "*Just do it. Follow your dream.*" Gun Denhart of Hanna Andersson reflects, "*Don't be afraid to fail and end up never trying.*" And this from Doris Christopher of The Pampered Chef, "*There may be obstacles, but follow your passion.*"

This success secret is shared as the last but it really is the start of everything. If you have a dream to own a business and a well-thought out plan, go forward, take action and don't look back. Perhaps your story will be included in the next volume of *Millionaire Women* success stories. Best wishes on your future success.

# Women's Resources

African-American Women
  Business Owners Association
  (AAWBOA)
3363 Alden Place NE
Washington, D.C. 20019
Phone: (202) 399-3645
Internet: www.blackpgs.com

American Association of
  University Women
AAUW Educational Foundation
1111Sixteenth Street NW
Washington, D.C. 20036
Phone: (800) 326-AAUW
Internet: www.aauw.org

American Business Women's
  Association (ABWA)
9100 Ward Parkway
Kansas City, MO 64114-0728
Phone: (800) 228-0007
Fax: (816) 361-4991
Internet: www.abwa.org

American Franchisee Association
53 West Jackson Boulevard
  Suite 205
Chicago, IL 60604
Phone: (312) 431-0545
Internet: www.franchisee.org

American Society of Women's
  Accountants (ASWA)
60 Revere Drive, Suite 500
Northbrook, IL 60062
Phone: (800) 326-2163 or (847)
  205-1029
Internet: www.aswa.org

Association for Women in
  Computing (AWC)
41 Sutter Street, Suite 1006
San Francisco, CA 94104
Phone: (415) 905-4663
Internet: www.awc-hq.org

Business and Professional Women
  USA (BPW/USA)
2012 Massachusetts Avenue, NW
Washington, D.C. 20036
Phone: (202) 293-1100
Fax: (202) 891-0298
www.bpwusa.org

Business Women's Network
  (BWN)
1990 M Street NW Suite 700
Washington, DC 20036
Phone: (800) 48WOMEN
Fax: (202) 833-1808
Internet: www.bwni.com

Canadian Association of Women
   Executives and Entrepreneurs
   (CAWEE)
3 Church Street, Suite 604
Toronto, Ontario
M5E 1M2
Phone: (416) 756-0000
Internet: www.cawee.net

Catalyst
120 Wall Street, 5th Floor
New York, New York 10005
Phone: (212) 514-7600
Internet: www.catalystwomen.org

Center for Women's Business
   Research
Formerly The National
   Foundation for Women
   Business Owner's (NFWBO)
1411 K Street, NW, Suite 1350
Washington, DC 20005-3407
Phone: (202) 638-3060
Fax: (202) 638-3064
Internet: www.nfwbo.org

Chamber of Commerce of the
   United States
1615 H Street NW
Washington D.C. 20062-2000
Phone: (202) 659-6000
Internet: www.uschamber.com

Child Care Action Campaign
   (CCAC)
330 7th Avenue, 14th Floor
New York, NY 10001
Phone: (212) 239-0138
Fax: (212) 268-6515
Internet:
   www.childcareaction.org

Committee of 200 (The)
625 N. Michigan Avenue,
   Suite 500
Chicago, Illinois, 60611
Phone: (312) 751-3477
Internet: www.c200.org

Direct Marketing Association
   (DMA)
1120 Avenue of the Americas
New York, NY 10036
Phone: (212) 768-7277
Internet: www.the-dma.org

Executive Women International
515South 700 East, Suite 2A
Salt Lake City, UT 84102
Phone: (801) 355-2800
Internet:
   www.executivewomen.org

FCEM (Les Femmes Chefs D'Entreprises Mondiales)
Im. Yasmine App 1.1
Les Berges du lac. 1053 Tunis
Tunisie
Telephone: +216 71 862 399
Internet: www.fcem.org

Institution of Women's Policy Research (IWPR)
1707 L Street NW, Suite 750
Washington, DC 20036
Phone: (202) 785-5100
Fax: (202) 833-4362
Internet: www.iwpr.org

International Franchise Association (IFA)
1350 New York Avenue NW
Washington, DC 20005
Phone: (202) 628-8000
Internet: www.franchise.org

Mothers at Home (MAH)
Family and Home Network
9493-C Silver King Court
Fairfax, VA 22031
Phone: (703) 352-1072
Internet: www.mah.org

Ms. Foundation for Women
120 Wall Street, 33rd Floor
New York, NY 10005
Phone: (212) 742-2300
Internet: www.ms.foundation.org

National Association for Female Executives, Inc. (NAFE)
P O Box 469031
Escondido, CA 92046
Phone: 800-634-NAFE
Internet: www.nafe.com

National Association of Women Business Owners (NAWBO)
1595 Spring Hill Road Suite 330
Vienna, VA 22182
Phone: (703) 506-3268
Fax: (703) 506-3266
Internet: www.nawbo.org

National Business Association (NBA)
P O Box 700728
Dallas, Texas 75370
Phone: (972) 458-0900 or (800) 456-0440
Internet: www.nationalbusiness.org

National Federation of Independent Business (NFIB)
600 Maryland Avenue SW, Suite 700
Washington, DC 20024
Phone: (800) NFIB-NOW
Internet: www.nfib.com

National Organization for Women
(NOW)
733 15th Street NW, 2nd Floor
Washington, DC 20005
Phone: (202) 628-8669
Internet: www.now.org

Office of Women's Business
Ownership
U.S. Small Business
Administration
409 3rd Street SW, 4th Floor
Washington, DC 20416
Phone: (202) 205-6673
Internet:
www.sba.gov/womeninbusiness

Service Corps of Retired
Executives (SCORE)
409 3rd Street SW, 6th Floor
Washington, D.C. 20024
Phone: (800) 634-0245
Internet: www.score.org

U.S. Small Business
Administration: SBA Answer
Desk
6302 Fairview Road Suite 300
Charlotte, NC 28210
Phone: 1 (800) UASK SBA
Internet: www.sba.gov

The White House Office of
Women's Initiatives and
Outreach
The White House
1600 Pennsylvania Avenue NW
Washington, DC 20500
Phone: (202) 456-1111
Internet:
www.whitehouse.gov/women

Women President's Organization
598 Broadway, 6th Floor
New York, NY 10012
Phone: (212) 941-8510
Internet:
www.womenpresidentsorg.com

Young President's Organization
(YPO)
451 South Decker Drive
Irving, TX 75062
Phone: (972) 650-4600 or (800)
773-7976
Internet: www.ypo.org

## The Millionaire Women Web Sites

Doris Christopher—
  The Pampered Chef
  www.pamperedchef.com

Gwen Willhite—Cookie Bouquet
  www.cookiesbydesign.com

Arlene Lenarz—Mary Kay
  Cosmetics
  www.marykay.com

Lane Nemeth—Discovery Toys
  www.discoverytoysinc.com

Lillian Vernon—Lillian Vernon
    www.lillianvernon.com

Patricia Miller & Barbara
  Baekgaard—Vera Bradley
  www.verabradley.com

Gun Denhart—Hanna Andersson
  www.hannaAndersson.com

Margaret Johnsson—
  The Johnsson Group
  www.thejohnssongroup.com

Mary Ellen Sheets—
  Two Men and a Truck
  www.twomen.com

Lorraine Tribe—Quest Personnel
  www.skilled.com.au

Mary Carroll—Schoolbelles
  www.schoolbelles.com

Stephanie Moss—Solutions Group
  www.solutionsgroup.co.za

Cynthia Jones—
  Jones Worley Design
  www.jonesworley.com

Victoria MacKenzie-Childs—
  MacKenzie Childs
  www.MacKenzie-Childs.com

Rian van Velzen-Bastiaansen—
  Natures Choice
  www.natures-choice.nl

Barbara Mowat—
  Home Business Report
  www.homebusinessreport.com

# References

## Chapter 1—The Millionaire Fascination

Lincoln Financial Group, Mendelsohn Media Research Inc., Yankelovich Partners and Wirthlin Worldwide Inc. (Private commission report), "More US Millionaires Than Ever Before" May, 2000.

Merrill Lynch and Gemini Consulting, (Worldwide private survey report), Online posting May 3, 2001 from the World Wide Web: http: www.yahoo.com.

Stanley, Thomas J., Ph.D. and Danko, William D., Ph.D. *The Millionaire Next Door*, New York: Pocket Books, 1996.

Stanley, Thomas. J. Ph.D. *TheMillionaire Mind*. Kansas City: Andrews McMeel, 2000.

*Yahoo!* Finance, "More US Millionaires than ever before - Study," Retrieved from the World Wide Web http:biz.yahoo.com May 3, 2000.

## Chapter 2—The First Woman Millionaire

Bundles, A'Lelia, *On Her Own Ground*. New York: Scribner, 2001.

Indiana Historical Society Archives, *Madam C.J. Walker Collection* (1867–1980). Collections: M399, OMB22, BV2667-2678.

## Chapter 3—Women in the Land of Plenty

Stanley, Thomas J. Ph.D. *The Millionaire Mind*, Kansas City: Andrews McMeel, 2000.

United States. Department of Labor. *Facts on Working Women,* "20 Facts on Women Workers," March 2000.

United States. Small Business Administration. *Women in Business 2001,* October 2001.

Center for Women's Business Research, *Women-Owned Business in 2002,* "Trends in the U.S. and Top Metro Areas," October 2001.

United States. Department of Labor Women's Bureau. *Facts on Working Women.* "Earnings Differences Between Men and Women", March 2000.

United States. Department of Labor Women's Bureau. *Facts on Working Women.* "20 Facts on Working Women", March 2000.

United States. Department of Labor Women's Bureau. *Facts on Working Women.* "Women at the Millennium, Accomplishments and Challenges Ahead", March 2000.

United States. Department of Labor. *Futurework Trends and Challenges for Work in the 21st Century,* 1999.

United States. Small Business Administration Online Women's Business Center. "Women and Small Business Startling New Statistics", Retrieved from the World Wide Web http: www.onlinewbc.org/docs/starting/new_stats.html. (June 23, 2000).

United States. Small Business Administration Office of Advocacy. *Women In Business: A Report on Statistical Information about Women-Owned Businesses,* October, 1998.

## *Chapter 4—The Pull to the Home*

United States. Small Business Administration Online Women's Business Center. *Trends in Home-Based Small Businesses,* Retrieved from the World Wide Web http: www.onlinewbc.org/docs/starting/hometrend. html. (June 23, 2000).

Burton, Linda, Dittmer, Janet, and Loveless, Cheri, *What's A Smart Woman Like You Doing At Home?* (Revised edition) Vienna: Mothers at Home, 1992.

Parlapiano, Ellen and Cobe, Patricia, *Mompreneurs,* New York: Putnam 2000.

Herman Group *Trend Alert,* "Staying At Home", Electronic bulletin posted on the World Wide Web www.alert@herman.net (June 28, 2000).

Mothers at Home: www.mah.org.

Clinton, Hilary, *It Takes A Village,* New York, Simon & Schuster 1996.

National Foundation for Women Business Owners/Center For Women's Business Research, *Key Facts,* Electronic bulletin posted on the World Wide Web http: www.nfwbo.org/key.html (October 5, 2001).

### Chapter Five—Doris Christopher

Christopher, Doris, *Come to the Table,* New York, Warner Books, 1999.

### Chapter Eight—Lane Nemeth

Nemeth, Lane, *Discovering Another Way,* Oregon, Beyond Words Publishing, 1999.

### Chapter Ten—Lillian Vernon

Vernon, Lillian, *An Eye For Winners,* New York, Harper, 1996.

### Success Cluster One

Briggs-Myers, Isabel, *Introduction to Type,* Palo Alto, Consulting Psychologists Press Fifth Edition 1993.

United States Department of Labor: www.dol.gov.

Keirsey, David and Bates, Marilyn, *Please Understand Me,* Del Mar, Prometheus Nemesis Books 1978.

Keirsey David, *Please Understand Me Part II,* Del Mar, Prometheus Nemesis Books 1998.

United States. Department of Labor Statistics. *The Occupational Outlook Handbook—2002–2003 Edition,* Washington D.C. 2002.

United States Bureau of Labor Statistics: www.bls.gov.

Nightingale-Conant: www.nightingale.com.

Successories: www.successories.com.

Hill, Napolean, *Think and Grow Rich,* New York, Fawcett Crest, Revised Edition 1960.

## Success Cluster Two

Senge, Peter, *The Fifth Discipline: The Art and Practice of the Learning Organization,* New York, Doubleday 1990.

Covey, Stephen, *The 7 Habits of Highly Effective People,* New York, Simon & Schuster, 1989.

Knowles, Elizabeth, *Oxford Dictionary of Quotations,* Oxford, Oxford University Press, Fifth Edition 1999.

Koplovitz, Kay, Speech to The City Club of Cleveland. "Empowering Women = Empowering the Economy," February 9, 2001.

## Success Cluster Three

*Forrester Online Retail Index,* November 2001. Electronic bulletin posted on the World Wide Web http: www.forrester.com March 3, 2002.

Boston Consulting Group, Silverstein, Stanger & Abdelmessih, "The Next Chapter In Business-To-Consumer E-Commerce", Retrieved April 14, 2002 from the World Wide Web: http:www.bcg.com.

Lizee, Joe, Interview with Internet specialist, Acero, Inc. strategic consulting and solutions provider, January 28, 2002.

Wing, Eliza, Interview with president of Cleveland.com, online news web site, January 19, 2001.

International Franchise Association: www.franchise.org

American Franchise Association: www.franchisee.org

Hauer, Richard, JD, Interview with pension specialist, Calfee, Halter & Griswold.

Kaufmann, Mel, *The Millionaire Handbook,* California 1999.

Hansen, Mark Victor, *Future Diary,* Newport Beach, Mark Victor Hansen Publishing Company - Ninth Edition 1997.

## Success Cluster Four

*Home Business Report,* Retrieved from the World Wide Web April 13, 2002. http:www.homebusinessreport.com.

# About the Author

**Jeanne Torrence Hauer** is a marketing professional and lecturer with over 20 years of experience working with both start-up and established organizations. Jeanne began her career working within an advertising agency giving her a broad view of business. Later, she created her own marketing consulting firm and then, ultimately moved into marketing responsibilities for an established corporation. She is currently a Regional Marketing Director for a Fortune 500 company.

Recognized for her marketing effectiveness and creativity, Jeanne has received numerous awards including recent recognition as Distinguished Sales & Marketing Professional of the Year-2001 from the Sales and Marketing Executives (SME) organization, and recognition as a 2001 Woman Rainmaker from *Northern Ohio Live* magazine. She is an Executive MBA graduate of Baldwin Wallace College.

Her insights about the experience of women in business are an outgrowth of her own experience, observation and research of personal success. Marketing professional, working wife and mother, "stay-at-home mom", volunteer, consultant/entrepreneur, and lecturer are among the roles Jeanne has filled over the course of her career. In 2003, she will be launching a monthly web newsletter through her website, **millionairewomenonline.com.**